Changed
by the
Master's
Touch

Changed by the Master's Touch

F. B. Meyer

Publisher's Note

We are pleased to offer this collection of classics by scholar F. B. Meyer. The three works were originally published as separate books, but they have been adapted and abridged so that today's reader may fully appreciate the author's insight into the lives and characters of these faithful followers of Christ. We pray that they will inspire and guide you into a closer walk with Him.

CHANGED BY THE MASTER'S TOUCH

F. B. Meyer

Copyright © 1985 by Whitaker House
Printed in the United States of America
ISBN: 0-88368-169-2

Edited by Diana L. Matisko and David L. Young

CONTENTS

PETER: THE DISCIPLE

PAUL: THE APOSTLE

PREFACE

The lives and characters of these men of faith have always held a great fascination for me, and I am thankful to have been permitted to write this book. But I am even more thankful for the hours of absorbing interest spent in the study of their portraits as given in the Gospels. I know of nothing that makes so pleasant a respite from life's pressures and strains than to bathe mind and spirit in the waters of Scriptural biography.

As the bridge between the Old and New Testaments—the close of the one and the beginning of the other—John the Baptist compels our admiration and respect. His spirit of humility and courage, his devotion to God, and his uncompromising loyalty to truth inspire us to be filled with the spirit and power of Elijah as he was.

Peter comes nearer to us than any of the other apostles. He is so human, so like ourselves, that we are encouraged that perhaps the Lord may also make much of our simple lives.

Paul's first conception of Jesus was in His risen glory. The radiant vision could never be erased from his memory, and it gave depth to his faith. For us, too, that vision waits.

When we battle against the lusts of the flesh, the fascinations of the world, and the power of the devil, no position has more certainty of victory than our resurrection standing and privilege. If the Master could do so much for these men, what may He do for you and me? By virtue of our union with Him, we must pray that the great Potter will make something even of our common clay.

F. B. Meyer

JOHN THE BAPTIST: THE FORERUNNER

Chapter 1

PROMISE OF THE PROPHET

In six brief months John the Baptist became the center of all Judea. Pharisees, Sadducees, soldiers, and publicans were amazed by his ministry. The Sanhedrin was forced to investigate his claims, the petty kings of Palestine trembled on their thrones, and he left a name and an influence that will never cease.

Few studies can better demonstrate the supreme glory of Christ than a thoughtful consideration of the story of the forerunner. Jesus and John were born at the same time and were surrounded by the same sacred traditions. But the parallel soon stops. John the Baptist is a representation of the noblest characteristics of the Jewish people, but Jesus is the Son of Man—there is a universality about Him. Each man's life was strenuous and short, bursting forth as they announced the Kingdom of God. In each case a handful of disciples bitterly mourned their master's death and took up the desecrated corpse to lay it in a tomb.

But there the parallel ends. The life purpose of the one culminated in his death; with the other, it only began. John's death was a martyrdom; Jesus' death was the sacrifice that put away the sin of the world. For John there was no immediate resurrection, but his Master saw no corruption. John's influence on the world has diminished as men have gotten further from his age, but Jesus is King of all ages. John was a burning torch lifted for a moment in the murky air, but Jesus *was the light!*

To read the picturesque pages of the gospels apart from some knowledge of contemporary history is to miss one of their deepest lessons—that such piety and goodness were set in the midst of a violent and dangerous age. Those times were by no means favorable to the cultivation of a spiritual life. The flock of God had long left the green pastures, and the wolf was coming. The national life reached its climax in the fall of Jerusalem, of which Jesus said there had been nothing—and would be nothing— like it in the history of the world.

Herod was on the throne. The temple that bore his name was the scene of priestly service and sacramental rites. The great national feasts of the Passover, Tabernacles, and Pentecost were celebrated with solemn pomp and attracted vast crowds from all the world. Synagogues were maintained with formal care, and crowds of scribes were engaged in a microscopic study of the law. But beneath this flowery surface was a desperate corruption.

Herod extorted immense revenues from the poorer classes and squandered them on his palaces and fortresses. He introduced Gentile customs and games everywhere and dared to place the Roman eagle on the main entrance of the temple. He pillaged David's tomb and set aside the great council of their nation. Religious leaders, men like Caiaphas and Annas, winked at the crimes of the secular power, as long as their prestige was secured.

But the darkest hour precedes the dawn, and Old Testament predictions must have been eagerly scanned by those that watched and waited. They could not doubt that the Messiah was near. The term of years foretold by Daniel had nearly expired. (See Daniel 10-12.) The Scepter had departed from Judah, and even Magi studying the dazzling glories of the eastern heavens had come to the conclusion that He was at hand who would bring again the Golden Age.

And so those loyal and loving souls that often spoke together must have felt that if the advent of the Lord whom they sought was near, then that of His messenger must be even nearer. They started at every footstep and listened for every voice. At any moment a voice might be heard crying, "Cast up, cast up the highway; gather out the stones; lift up a standard for the people. Say ye to the daughter of Zion, Behold, thy salvation cometh" (Isaiah 62:10-11). Those anticipations were realized in the birth of John the Baptist.

Chapter 2

THE HOUSE OF ZACHARIAS

God has always had His hidden ones. While the world has been rent by war and ravaged by fire and sword, these have heard His call to shut themselves in until the storm has spent its fury. Among these were the priest Zacharias and his wife Elisabeth.

Zacharias meant "God's remembrance" as though he were to be a perpetual reminder to his people of what God had promised—and to God of what they were expecting from His hand. *Elisabeth* meant "God's oath" as though her people were perpetually appealing to those covenant promises.

Zacharias was a priest, and twice a year he journeyed to Jerusalem to fulfill his office for six days and two Sabbaths. More than 20,000 priests were settled in Judea at this time. Many of them were like those Malachi denounced as degrading the Temple. The general character of the priesthood was tainted by the corruption of the times, and, as a class, they were blind leaders of the blind. Not a few, however, were evidently deeply religious men, for we find that "a great company of the priests" (Acts 6:7), after the crucifixion, believed in Christ and joined His followers. In this class was Zacharias, who, with his wife, is described as being "righteous before God" (Luke 1:6).

The phrases are evidently selected with care. Many are righteous before *men*, but they were *"righteous before God."* Their life was regulated by a careful observance of the ceremonial and the moral law. It is evident from the many quotations in the song of Zacharias that the Scriptures were reverenced in their home. Because they lived up to the fullest limit of their knowledge of the will of God, they were blameless and harmless children of God in the midst of a crooked and perverse generation.

But they lived under the shadow of a great sorrow. "They had no child, because that Elisabeth was barren, and they both were now well stricken in years" (Luke 1:7). They would, therefore, count themselves under the frown of God; and Elisabeth especially felt that a reproach lay on her. A clue to the anguish of her soul is furnished by her reflection, when she recognized the divine intervention on her behalf and cried, "Thus hath the Lord dealt with me in the days wherein he looked on me, to take away my reproach among men" (Luke 1:25).

If it had not been for this sorrow, they might never have been qualified to receive the first tidings of the near approach of the Messiah. *Sorrow* opens our eyes and allows us to see visions within the veil that cannot be described by those who have not wept. Shrink not from sorrow. It endures but for the night; joy comes in the morning. (See Psalms 30:5.) It may be caused by apparently fruitless prayer. Beneath its pressure, heart and flesh may faint. Yet the Lord shows His lovingkindness in the morning and assures us that our prayer is heard. (See Psalm 92:2.)

Zacharias stood alone in the holy shrine, while the incense he had strewn on the glowing embers rose in fragrant clouds. "And there appeared unto him an angel of the Lord standing on the right side of the altar of incense" (Luke 1:11). It was Gabriel, who stood in the presence of God, that had been sent to declare the good tidings that Zacharias' prayer was heard and that his wife would bear a son. He would be called John and would be a Nazarite from birth, filled with the Holy Spirit. He would inherit the spirit and power of Elijah and go before the Christ to prepare His way. (See Luke 1:11-17.)

When Zacharias finally came out of the temple, he was dumb. He had not believed the archangel's words. Perhaps he might learn in silence and solitude the full purposes of God.

With the light of that glory on his face and those sweet notes of *"Fear not"* ringing in his heart, Zacharias departed to his house. But that day was long remembered by the people as a prelude to the time when their blessings would come from Calvary.

Then the great High Priest would declare from heaven the ancient words:

"The Lord bless thee, and keep thee: The Lord make his face shine upon thee, and be gracious unto thee. The Lord lift up his countenance upon thee, and give thee peace" (Numbers 6:24-26).

Chapter 3

SCHOOLS AND SCHOOLMASTERS

Zacharias and Elisabeth had probably stopped praying for a child. No heaven-sent sign assured them that their prayer was being answered, and nature seemed to utter a final, "No." But suddenly, the angel of God broke into their life and announced that their prayer had been heard.

On his arrival home, the aged priest informed his wife of all that had happened. She found no difficulty in accepting the divine assurance. During her five months of seclusion, she believed that her child would become all that his name was supposed to signify: *the gift of Jehovah.*

Month succeeded month, and Zacharias neither heard nor spoke. His friends had to make signs to him, for unbelief has the effect of shutting man out of the enjoyment of life and hindering his usefulness. He was a good man, well versed in the history of his people. His soul, as we learn from his song, was full of noble pride in the great and glorious past. (See Luke 1:68-79.) He could believe that when Abraham and Sarah were past age a child had been born to *them,* but he could not believe that such a blessing could also fall on him.

Is that the point where *our faith* staggers? We can believe in the wonder-working power of God on the distant horizon of the past, or on the equally distant horizon of the future; but that He should have a definite and particular care for *our* life or that *our* prayer should touch Him—this staggers us, and we feel it is too good to be true.

Shut off from communication with the outer world, Zacharias' spirit became charged with holy emotion that waited for the first opportunity of expression. Such an opportunity came at last. One day an eager and enthusiastic throng of relatives and friends gathered to congratulate the aged pair, perform the initial rite of Judaism, and name the infant boy that lay in his mother's arms.

In their perplexity at the mother's insistence that the babe's name should be John—none of his kindred were known by that name—they appealed to his father. With a trembling hand, he inscribed on a writing tablet, "His name *is* John." As he broke the chains of unbelief, "his mouth was opened immediately, and his tongue loosed, and he spake, and praised God. And fear came on all that dwelt round about them" (Luke 1:64-65). These sayings quickly became the theme of conversation throughout the hill-country of Judea. People wondered in their hearts, saying, "What manner of child shall this be!" (Luke 1:66).

"And the child grew, and waxed strong in spirit" (Luke 1:80). There were several remarkable influences operating on this young life.

John's father was a priest. His earliest memories would register the frequent absence of his father. On Zacharias' return, with eagerness the boy would drink in a recital of all that had happened in the city! We can imagine how the three would sit together and talk of Zion, their chief joy. No wonder when he looked at Jesus, he pointed to Him and said, "Behold the Lamb of God" (John 1:29). From childhood, his young mind had been saturated with thoughts of sacrifice.

His parents would take him to the great festivals, where his boyish eyes opened upon the stately temple and the solemn pomp of the Levitical ceremonies. He would also be taught carefully in the Holy Scriptures. The song of Zacharias reveals a vivid and realistic familiarity with the prophecies of the Scriptures. As the parents recited them to his infant mind, they would emphasize them with personal references.

There were also the associations of the surrounding country. The story of Abraham would often be recited in the proximity of Machpelah's sacred cave. (See Genesis 23.) David's career could not be unfamiliar to John, who lived near the haunts of the shepherd-psalmist. The exploits of the Maccabees would stir his soul as his parents recounted the deeds of Judas and his brethren, who had revived the ancient Hebrew faith in one last glorious outburst.

How strong are the impressions of the home! Is the father willing to be the companion of his child, answering his questions and directing the gradual unfolding of his mind? How often is the Bible opened and explained? These questions are vital to the right nurture and direction of children who can only grow strong in spirit when early influences unite in the same direction.

John was a Nazarite. The angel who announced his birth foretold that he should drink neither wine nor strong drink from his birth but that he should be filled with the Holy Spirit. "John," said our Lord, "came neither eating nor drinking" (Matthew 11:18). This abstinence from all intoxicants was a distinct sign of the Nazarite, together with the unshorn locks and the refusal of contact with death. In some cases, the vow of the Nazarite could be taken for a time; or, as in the case of Samson, Samuel, and John, it could be for life. But whether for shorter or longer, the Nazarite kept himself for the service of God.

This lifestyle would give a direction and purpose to the lad's thoughts and anticipations. He would realize that he was set apart for a great mission in life and would acquire self-restraint and self-mastery.

On each of us rests the vow of separation by right of our union with the Son of God, who was holy, harmless, undefiled, and separate from sinners. He bore *our* reproach and was put to death on the cross. His death has made a lasting break between His followers and the rest of men. We are crucified to the world, and the world is crucified to us. Let us not taste the intoxicating joys that the children of the present age indulge in. Let us allow no Delilah to pass her scissors over our locks, and let us have no fellowship with the unfruitful works of darkness. Instead, let us be separate, not touching any unclean thing.

But while we put away all that injures our own life, or the lives of others, let us be very careful to draw the line where God would draw it. It is important to remember that while the motto of the old covenant was *exclusion,* that of the new is *inclusion.* Christ has come to sanctify life. Disciples are not to be taken out of the world but kept from its evil. Natural instincts are not to be crushed but transfigured.

This is the great contrast between the Baptist and the Son of Man. The Nazarite would have felt it a sin against the law of his office to touch anything pertaining to the vine. Christ performed His first miracle by providing wine in abundance. John would have lost all sanctity had he touched the bodies of the dead or the flesh of a leper. Christ would touch a bier and pass His hands over the seared flesh of the leper. We catch a glimpse of our Lord's meaning when He affirms that, although John was the greatest born of women, the least in the Kingdom of heaven is greater than he.

The child "was in the deserts till the day of his shewing unto Israel'' (Luke 1:80). Zacharias and Elisabeth probably died when John was quite young.

But the boy had grown into adolescence and was able to care for himself, and "the hand of the Lord was with him" (Luke 1:66).

Beneath the guidance and impulse of that hand he passed forth into the great and terrible wilderness of Judea. Void of all animal life, except a chance vulture or fox, it is mostly a waste of sand, swept by wild winds. In this land John supported himself by eating locusts—the tops of vegetation—and wild honey, which abounded in the crevices of the rocks. For clothing, he was content with a coat of coarse camel's hair and a girdle of skin about his loins. A simple cave was his home.

Can we wonder that under such a regimen he grew strong? We become weak by continual contact with our fellowmen. But in loneliness and solitude, wherein we meet God, we become strong. God's strong men are rarely clothed in soft raiment or found in kings' courts.

He who is filled and taught, as John was, by the Holy Spirit is strengthened by might in the inner man. All things are possible to him that believes. They who wait on the Lord shall renew their strength, and they who know God are strong and do great deeds.

Chapter 4

PROPHET OF THE HIGHEST

"Thou, child, shalt be called the prophet of the Highest" (Luke 1:76)—thus Zacharias addressed his infant son as he lay in the midst of his wondering neighbors and friends. What a thrill of ecstasy quivered in the words! Four hundred years had passed since Malachi, the last great Hebrew prophet. But now as the angel proclaimed the advent of a prophet, hope revived. Our Lord confirmed Zacharias' words when He said that John had been a prophet. "But what went ye out for to see?" He asked. "A prophet? yea, I say unto you, and more than a prophet" (Matthew 11:9).

The Hebrew word that stands for *prophet* is derived from a root word signifying "to boil or bubble over" and suggests a fountain bursting from the heart. It is a mistake to confine the word to the prediction of coming events. The prophet is borne along by the stream of divine indwelling and inflowing, whether he utters the truth for the moment or anticipates the future. "God spake in the prophets" (Hebrews 1:1, Revised Version). And when they were conscious of His mighty moving within, woe to them if they did not utter it in burning words.

As the voice of Old Testament prophecy ceased, it foretold with its last breath that it would be followed by a new and glorious revival of the most noble traditions of the prophetic office: "Behold, I will send you Elijah the prophet before the coming of the great and dreadful day of the Lord. And he shall turn the heart of the fathers to the children, and the heart of the children to their fathers, lest I come and smite the earth with a curse" (Malachi 4:5-6).

The prophecies had given a forecast of John's career. From his childhood they had been reiterated by his parents, who would never weary of reciting them. How often he would ponder the reference to himself in the great Messianic prediction: "Comfort ye, comfort ye my people, saith your God. . . . The voice of him that crieth in the wilderness, Prepare ye the way of the Lord, make straight in the desert a highway for our God" (Isaiah 40:1,3). There was no doubt as to the relevance of those words to himself. (See Luke 1:76; Matthew 3:3.) It must have mightily influenced his character and ministry.

There was also that striking anticipation by Malachi that directly suggested Elijah as his model. The great figure of the prophet was ever before the mind of the growing youth. His choice of the lonely wilderness and the mantle of camel's hair was probably suggested by the personal characteristics that were so familiar in the Prophet of Fire.

But the mind of the forerunner also must have been greatly exercised by the lawlessness and crime that involved all classes of his countrymen in a common condemnation. Tidings of the evil that was overflowing the land were constantly coming to the ears of his eager soul, filling it with horror and dismay. The idea that lies beneath the fasting of so many of God's servants has been that of an overwhelming sorrow. And this was the thought that penetrated John. On one hand was his agonizing conviction of the sin of Israel; and on the other hand was the belief that the Messiah must be near. The pressure of the burden increased on him until he was forced to cry from his soul: "Repent ye: for the kingdom of heaven is at hand" (Matthew 3:2).

In addition to these, the vision of God must have been especially granted to him while he sojourned in those lonely wilds. He became accustomed to detect His presence and hear His voice. The still, small voice that had fallen on the ear of Elijah thrilled his soul.

In this we may have some share. It is permitted to us also to have revealed to us things that eye has not seen, or ear heard, or the heart of man conceived. (See 1 Corinthians 2:9.) We are to be God's *witnesses* to the uttermost parts of the earth. God demands not advocates but witnesses; and we must see the glory of His light.

These are the three signs of a prophet: vision, a deep conviction of sin and impending judgment, and the gushing forth of moving speech. Each of these was apparent in an extreme degree in John the Baptist.

Chapter 5

THE MINISTRY OF BAPTISM

Thirty years had left their mark on John. Zacharias and Elisabeth had been carried to their grave by other hands than those of the young Nazarite. The story of his miraculous birth and the expectations it had aroused had almost died out. For many years John had been living in the desolate wilderness that extends from Hebron to the western shores of the Dead Sea. From nature, from the Scriptures, and from direct fellowship with God, he had received revelations given only to those who can stand the strain of discipline in the school of solitude. He had carefully pondered also the signs of the times. John's heart was filled with the advent of Him who was soon to be manifested to Israel.

At last the moment arrived for him to utter the mighty burden that pressed upon him. "The word of God came unto John, the son of Zacharias in the wilderness" (Luke 3:2). It was as though a spark had fallen on dry timber. The tidings quickly spread that in the wilderness of Judea was one whose burning eloquence was the same as Isaiah's or Ezekiel's. Instantly people began to flock to him from all sides. "Then went out to him Jerusalem, and all Judaea, and all the region round about Jordan" (Matthew 3:5).

Many things accounted for John's immense popularity. The office of the prophet was almost obsolete. The oldest living man could not remember having seen anyone who had ever spoken to a prophet. Moreover, John was evidently sincere. His independence made men feel that whatever he said was inspired by his direct contact with things as they are. He spoke what he knew and testified what he had seen. His conviction was unmistakable.

Above all, he appealed to their *moral convictions* and expressed them. The people *knew* that they were not as they should be. For a long time this consciousness had been gaining ground. Now they flocked around the man who revealed their wickedness and indicated the course of action they should adopt. In his direct appeal to the heart and conscience, the servant of God exerts his supreme power. A man may shrink from the preaching of repentance, yet, if it tells him the truth about himself, he will be irresistibly attracted to hear the voice that torments his soul.

John saw many Pharisees and Sadducees coming to be baptized. Their presence appears to have caused him some surprise. "O generation of vipers, who hath warned you to flee from the wrath to come?" (Matthew 3:7). His reference to them suggests that they came as critics. They were unwilling to surrender the leadership of the religious life of Israel and were anxious to keep in touch with the new movement until they could sap its vitality into the channels of their own influence.

But it is quite likely that in many cases there were deeper reasons. *The Pharisees* were the ritualists and formalists of their day, but the mere externals of religion will never permanently satisfy the soul made in the likeness of God. Ultimately it will turn from them with an insatiable desire for the living God. As for *the Sadducees,* they were materialists of their time. Disgusted and outraged by the trifling of the literalists of Scriptural interpretation, the Sadducee denied that there was an eternal world and a spiritual state. But mere denial can never satisfy the soul. Nature's instincts are stronger than reason. It was no surprise, then, that these two great classes were largely represented in the crowds that gathered on the banks of the Jordan.

The Kingdom of heaven is at hand. To a Jew that phrase meant a return to the days when God Himself was Lawgiver and King. Daniel had foreseen a time when one like a son of man would come to the Ancient of Days to receive a dominion that would not pass away and a Kingdom that would not be destroyed! (See Daniel chapter 7.) Surely all these anticipations were on the eve of fulfillment. The long-expected Messiah was at hand, and here was the forerunner described by Isaiah, the prophet, saying, "The voice of one crying in the wilderness, pre-

pare ye the way of the Lord, Make his paths straight"
(Mark 1:3).

But his hearers must have doubted when they
heard the young prophet's description of the conditions and accompaniments of the Kingdom. Instead of expanding on the material glory of the
Messianic period, he insisted on the fulfillment of
certain preliminary requirements that lifted the
whole conception of the reign to a new level. The
inward and spiritual was to take precedence over
the outward and material. Unless a man is born from
above, he cannot see the Kingdom of God.

No outward circumstances can bring about true
blessedness. Life must be centered in Christ if it is
to be in harmony with heaven's bliss. We can never
be at rest or happy while we expect to find our life
in outward circumstances. Righteousness is blessedness. Where the King is enthroned within the
heart, the Kingdom is in the soul.

Alongside the proclamation of the Kingdom was
the uncompromising insistence of *"the wrath to
come."* John saw that the advent of the King would
bring inevitable suffering to those who were living
in self-indulgence and sin.

There would be careful discrimination. He who
was coming would carefully discern between those
who served God and those who did not. This would
be a very careful process, with sheep on one side
and goats on the other. And in every age Jesus Christ
is the deciding factor, and our attitude toward Him
reveals the true quality of the soul.

There would also be a period of probation. The Jewish people had become sadly unfruitful; but a definite period was to intervene—three years of Christ's ministry and thirty years beside—before the threatened judgment fell. All this while the axe lay ready for its final stroke; but only when all hope of reformation was abandoned was it driven home, and the nation crashed to its doom.

This may be the case with you. You have been planted on a favorable site and have drunk in the rain and sunshine of God's providence, but what fruit have you yielded in return? How have you repaid the heavenly Husbandman? He has looked for grapes, and you have brought forth only wild grapes; He may well remove you from the stewardship that you have used for your own benefit instead of His glory.

The fire of John's preaching had its primary fulfillment in the awful disasters that befell the Jewish people and culminated in the siege and fall of Jerusalem. The handful of believers that had been gathered by Christ and His disciples were accounted worthy to escape all those things and stand before the Son of Man. But the unbelieving mass of the Jewish people were discovered to be worthless chaff and were assigned to the terrible fires that have left a scar on Palestine to this day.

But there was a deeper meaning. The wrath of God avenges itself not on nations but on individual sinners. "He that believeth not the Son shall not see life; but the wrath of God abideth on him" (John

3:36). The penalty of sin is inevitable. "The wages of sin is death" (Romans 6:23). Even if we suggest that many of the expressions referring to the ultimate fate of the ungodly are symbolic, it must be granted that they have counterparts in the spiritual realm that are terrible to endure.

The nature of the soul is more highly organized than that of the body. Fire to the body is easy to bear in comparison with certain forms of suffering that the heart and soul are sometimes exposed to. And if we are capable of suffering so acutely from remorse, shame, ingratitude, and misrepresentation, what are the possibilities of pain in that other life? Jesus said, "These shall go away into everlasting punishment" (Matthew 25:46). He considered judgment so terrible that it would have been better for the sufferers if they had never been born.

All the great preachers have seen the fearful results of sin. These threw Brainerd into a dripping sweat while praying for his Indians in the woods; these forced tears from Whitefield as he preached to thousands; these burn in the memorable sermon by Jonathan Edwards, "Sinners in the hands of an angry God." But God is not confined to any one method, and the preaching of the late D.L. Moody was especially steeped in the love of God.

A lack of vision of the fate of the godless and disobedient weakens much present-day preaching. Only when we modern preachers have seen sin *as God sees it* and begin to pluck men out of the fire will we see the effects that followed the preaching of John the Baptist. Soldiers, publicans, Pharisees, and scribes crowded around him, saying, "What shall we do?" (Luke 3:10).

All John's preaching led up to the demand for repentance. The word most often on his lips was *Repent!* It was not enough to plead direct descent from Abraham. God could raise up children to Abraham from the stones of the river bank. There must be the renunciation of sin, a definite turning to God, and the bringing forth of fruit. In no other way could the people be prepared for the coming of the Lord.

Chapter 6

THE FRUIT OF REPENTANCE

John represents a phase of teaching and influence through which we must pass if we are to discover and appreciate the grace of Christ. A preparatory work has to be done. Pride and self-will have to be leveled, crooked and devious ways have to be straightened, and ruggedness has to be smoothed before we can fully behold the glory of God in the face of Jesus Christ. Our realization of the fullness and glory of the Lamb of God will be in proportion to the thoroughness and permanence of our repentance.

But we must guard ourselves here; repentance is not a species of good work that must be performed in order to merit the grace of Christ. It must not be viewed apart from faith in the Savior. Although "God commandeth all men everywhere to repent" (Acts 17:30), yet Jesus is exalted to give "repentance and the remission of sins" (Luke 24:47).

Repentance, according to the literal rendering of the Greek word, is "a change of mind." It is a change in the attitude of the will. The unrepentant soul chooses its own way and will, regardless of the law of God. "The carnal mind is enmity against God: for it is not subject to the law of God, neither indeed can be. So then they that are in the flesh cannot please God" (Romans 8:7-8). But in repentance the soul changes its attitude. Habits may rebel and inclinations and emotions may shrink back, but the will has made its secret decision and has begun to turn to God.

It cannot be too strongly emphasized that *repentance is an act of the will*. It brings the consciousness that certain ways of life grieve God and strengthen the desire to turn from them and seek Him.

Repentance may be accounted as the other side of faith. *Repentance* stands for the desire and *choice* to turn from sin, and *faith* stands for the desire and *choice* to turn to God. We must be willing to turn from sin and our own righteousness—that is *repentance;* and we must be willing to be saved by God, in His own way, and must come to Him for that purpose—that is *faith*.

We must turn away from our own efforts to save ourselves. These are, in the words of the prophet, "filthy rags." (See Isaiah 64:6.) Nothing apart from the words of the Savior can help the soul, which must meet the scrutiny of eternal justice and purity.

Repentance is produced especially by the presentation of the claims of Christ. We suddenly awake to realize what He is, how He loves, how much we are missing, and the gross ingratitude with which we respond to His agony and bloody sweat.

At other times repentance is influenced by the preaching of John the Baptist. Then our faith in our hereditary position and privilege is shattered by the preacher. We see the entire fabric of its vain confidences and hopes crumbling like a cloud-palace and turn from it all.

For purposes of clear thinking it is well to discriminate in our use of the words *repentance* and *penitence. Repentance* is an act of the will, when it turns from dead works to serve the living and true God; *penitence* refers to the emotions that are powerfully experienced as the years pass. We repent once but are penitent always. We repent in the will and are penitent in the heart. We repent and believe the gospel; we believe the gospel of the Son of Man and, as we look on Him whom our sins have pierced, we mourn.

Be sure to open your heart to John the Baptist's piercing voice. Let him fulfill his ministry. See that you do not reject the counsel of God as it proceeds from his lips, but expose your soul to its searching scrutiny and allow it to be free and uninterrupted. He comes to prepare the way of the Lord and to make a highway for our God through the desert of our nature.

They "were baptized of him in Jordan, confessing their sins" (Matthew 3:6). Beneath the pressure of remorse and bitterness of spirit, men stood up and confessed their deeds. (See Acts 19:17-20.) The air was laden with the cries and sighs of the stricken multitudes, who beheld their sin for the first time in the light of eternity. The flames of "the wrath to come" cast their searching light on practices that, in ignorance and neglect, had passed without special notice.

Upon that river bank, men not only confessed to God but probably also to one another. Life-long feuds were reconciled, old quarrels were settled, and hands grasped hands for the first time in years.

Confession is an essential sign of a genuine repentance, and without it forgiveness is impossible. "He that covereth his sin shall not prosper; but whoso confesseth and forsaketh them shall have mercy" (Proverbs 28:13). "If we confess our sins, he is faithful and just to forgive us our sins, and to cleanse us from all unrighteousness" (1 John 1:9). As long as we keep silence, our bones grow old through our inward anguish. But on confession there is immediate relief.

Confess your sin to God! Some undetected or unconfessed sin may be shutting out the rays of the true sun. Excuse nothing. Do not speak of mistakes of judgment but of lapses of heart and will. Do not be content with a general confession; be specific. Begin at the beginning and go steadily through. Directly, the divine voice is heard assuring us that our sins, which are many, are put away as far as the east is from the west and cast into the depths of the sea.

Confession should not be made to God alone

when sins that have injured and alienated others are in question. If our brother has anything *against us,* we must find him, while our gift is left unpresented at the altar, and first be reconciled to him. But the only sins we are justified in confessing to our brother are those that we have committed against him. All else must be told to Jesus, that great High Priest, whose confessional is always open and whose pure ear can receive our dark, sad stories without stain or soil.

You will never get right with God until you are right with man. It is not enough to confess wrong-doing; you must be prepared to make amends as far as it lies in your power. Sin is not a light thing, and it *must* be dealt with, root and branch.

The cleansing property of water has given baptism a religious significance. Men have conceived of sin as a foul stain upon the heart and have laid their petitions for its removal in words derived from the use of water: "Purge me with hyssop, and I shall be clean: wash me, and I shall be whiter than snow" (Psalm 51:7). They have longed to feel that as the body was delivered from pollution, so the soul was freed from stain.

It is not necessary to discuss the source from which the Baptist derived his baptism—some say it was from the habits of the Essenes or the practice of the Rabbis. It is enough for us to remember that he was *sent* to baptize, that the idea of his baptism was "from heaven," and that in his hands the rite assumed altogether new and important functions.

It meant death and burial, as far as the past was concerned, and resurrection to a new and better future. Dying to the things that were behind, the soul was urged to press on, assured that God had accepted its confession and choice and was waiting to receive it graciously.

It is easy to see how all this appealed to the people, and especially touched the hearts of young men. When tidings reached them of this strange new preacher, they left all and streamed to the Jordan valley and stood fascinated by the spell of his words.

One by one, they made themselves known to him and became his loyal friends and disciples. We are familiar with the names of one or two of them, who afterwards left their earlier master to follow Christ. Of the rest we know nothing, except that he taught them to fast and pray, and that they clung to their great teacher until they bore his headless body to the grave.

How much this meant to John! To have the allegiance and love of these noble youths must have been a blessing to his soul. But from them all he repeatedly turned his gaze, as though he were looking for someone to emerge from the crowd, the sound of whose voice would give him deep and rich fulfillment—it would be the voice of the Christ.

Chapter 7

BAPTISM OF THE MESSIAH

John's conviction that the Messiah was near grew stronger, and this conviction became a revelation. The Holy Spirit, who filled him, taught him. He began to see the outlines of His Person and work. As John thought about Him, His personality glimmered on his inner consciousness, and he could even describe the Holy Spirit to others.

He conceived of the coming King as a woodsman, laying His axe at the root of the trees; as a husbandman, fan in hand to winnow the threshing floor; as a baptist, prepared to plunge all faithful souls in His cleansing fires; and as the Ancient of Days, who must be preferred before him in order of precedence because He was before him in the eternal glory of His being. (See John 1:15-30.)

John insisted that he was not worthy to perform the most menial service for Him whose advent he announced: "One mightier than I cometh, the latchet of whose shoes I am not worthy to unloose" (Luke 3:16).

John was not only humble in self-esteem but also in his appreciation of the results of his work. It was only preparatory. His simple mission was to bid the people to believe in Him who would come after him. He was the morning star ushering in the day, destined to fade in the glory of the dawn that flooded the eastern sky.

For thirty years the Son of Man had been busy in the ordinary routine of a village carpenter. Often He must have felt the strong attraction of the great world of men that He loved. The wild winds must have often borne to Him the wail of broken hearts asking Him to hasten to their relief. But He waited until the time was fulfilled that had been fixed in the eternal council chamber.

As soon, however, as the rumors of the Baptist's ministry reached Him, He knew that the porter had taken up his position at the door of the sheepfold, ready to admit the true Shepherd. (See John 10:3.) He could hesitate no longer but must tear Himself away from Nazareth and take the road that would end at Calvary.

Tradition locates the scene of John's baptism as near Jericho, where the water is shallow and opens out into large lagoons. But some, inferring that Nazareth was within a day's journey of this notable spot, place it nearer the southern end of the Lake of Galilee.

It may have been in the late afternoon when Jesus arrived. Luke suggests that all the people had been baptized for the day. (See Luke 3:21.) Perhaps the crowds had dispersed, and the great prophet was alone with one or two of his disciples. Or, Jesus may have arrived when the Jordan banks were alive with eager multitudes. In either case, a sudden and remarkable change passed over the Baptist's face as he beheld his kinsman standing there.

John said, "I knew Him not" (John 1:31), but this does not mean that he had no acquaintance whatever with his relative. It is more natural to suppose that the cousins had often met, as boys and afterwards. But the Baptist had never realized that Jesus was the Messiah whose advent he was sent to announce. It had never occurred to him that this simple village carpenter could be He of whom Moses in the Law and the Prophets wrote. In this sense John could truly say, "I knew Him not."

An indescribable apprehension stole over John's lofty nature. He knew men; his eye had searched their hearts as he heard them confess their sins, and he could tell what was in them. He was a connoisseur of souls. Among all the pearls that had passed through his hands, none had seemed so rare and pure as this. An indefinable majesty in this man was appreciated by John. "I have need to be baptized of thee, and comest thou to me?" (Matthew 3:14).

"Suffer it to be so now: for thus it becometh us to fulfill all righteousness" (Matthew 3:15). With these words our Lord overruled the objections of His loyal and faithful forerunner. This is the first recorded utterance of Christ after a silence of more than twenty years. He did not explain why the greater should be baptized by the less or why a rite that confessed sin was required for one who was absolutely sinless. It was enough to appeal to the Baptist as His associate in a necessary act, therefore claiming their common obedience. *"It becometh us* (you and me) *to fulfill all righteousness."*

In His baptism, our Lord acknowledged the divine authority of the forerunner. John was the last and greatest of the prophets and was to close the Old Testament era: "The prophets and the law prophesied until John" (Matthew 11:13). As the representative of Elijah the prophet, John occupied a unique position, and it was as an acknowledgement of his office that Jesus sought baptism at his hands.

John's baptism was the inauguration of the Kingdom of heaven. It was the outward and visible sign that Judaism was unavailing for the deepest needs of the spirit of man and that a new and more spiritual system was about to take its place. Christ said, in effect, "I, too, though King, obey the law of the Kingdom and bow My head, that I may pass forward to My throne."

There was probably a deeper reason still. The Jordan River was contaminated by the evil that is in the world through lust and deserved the wages of sin—death! Jesus' baptism was His formal identification with our fallen and sinful race, although He knew no sin for Himself. He could challenge the minutest inspection of his enemies: "Which of you convinceth me of sin?" (John 8:46).

Was He baptized because He needed to repent or

to confess His sins? No! He was as pure as the bosom of God, from which He came, but He needed to be made sin that we might be made the righteousness of God in Him. When the paschal lamb had been chosen by the head of a Jewish household, it was customary to take it, three days before it would be offered, to have it sealed with the temple seal. So our Lord, three years before His death, had to be set apart and sealed by the direct act of the Holy Spirit through the mediation of John the Baptist. "Him hath God the Father sealed" (John 6:27).

Nothing is more attractive than when a strong man yields to another, accepts a deeper interpretation of duty than he had before, and prepares to set aside his strong convictions before the tender pleading of a still, soft voice. Yield to Christ. Allow Him to have His way. Take His yoke, and be meek and lowly of heart—you *will* find rest.

The revelation of Jesus as the Christ was not given to any but John. It was apparently a private sign given to him, through which he might be informed of the Messiah's identity. John's own statements seem to point clearly in this direction. He says, "I knew him not" (i.e., as Messiah), "but he that sent me to baptize with water, the same said unto me, upon whom thou shalt see the Spirit descending, and remaining on him, the same is he which baptizeth with the Holy Ghost. And I saw and have recorded that this is the Son of God" (John 1:33-34).

What a manifestation was here! As Jesus emerged from the water, the sign for which John had been eagerly waiting was granted. He had believed he would see it but had never thought to see it granted to one so near akin to himself. We never expect the great God to come to *us!* The Spirit descended in visible shape—as a dove might—and alighted on the Holy One, who stood there fresh from His baptism.

The stress of the narrator was that the Spirit not only came but *remained*. Here was the miracle of miracles, that He should be willing to *abide* in any human temple. Here was an ark into which this second Noah might pull in the fluttering dove.

The voice of God from heaven proclaimed that Jesus of Nazareth was His beloved Son, in whom He was well pleased. The Baptist could have no further doubt that the Lord whom his people sought had come to His temple. "John bare record, saying, I saw the Spirit descending from heaven like a dove, and it abode upon him" (John 1:32).

How much that designation meant to Christ! It was His Pentecost and His consecration and dedication to His life-work. The Spirit of the Lord was upon Him, and He was anointed to preach. John knew that his mission was nearly fulfilled. He had opened the gate to the true Shepherd and must soon give to Him all charge of the flock. Jesus must increase while he decreased. The Sun had risen, and the day-star began to wane.

Chapter 8

WITNESS OF THE LIGHT

The baptism and revelation of Christ had a marvelous effect on the ministry of John the Baptist. Previous to that memorable day, the burden of his teaching had been repentance and confession of sin. But afterwards, the whole force of his testimony was the person and glory of the Shepherd of Israel. He understood that, for the remainder of his brief ministry, he must bend all his strength to announcing to the people the claims of Jesus.

"There was a man sent from God, whose name was John. The same came for a witness, to bear witness of the Light, that all men through him might believe. He was not that Light, but was sent to bear witness of that Light" (John 1:6-8).

When the apostle John used the word "Jews," he invariably means the Sanhedrin. (See John 1:19.) John the Baptist had become famous, and his influence was commanding. He could not be ignored by the religious leaders of the time. In their hearts they derided him for his preaching of repentance, and his unmeasured denunciation of them as a brood of vipers was not to be tolerated. But they would not meet him in the open field. Instead, they sent a delegation to extract some admission from his lips that would furnish them with ground for action.

The group of grey-beards, representatives of a decadent religion, challenged the prophet with the inquiry, "Who art thou?" (John 1:19). There was a great silence. Men were prepared to believe anything of the eloquent young preacher: "The people were in expectation, and all men mused in their hearts of John, whether he were the Christ" (Luke 3:15). If he had given the least encouragement to their dreams and hopes, they would have swept like a wild hurricane against the Roman occupation and been wiped out in blood. But "he confessed, and denied not; but confessed, I am not the Christ" (John 1:20).

A second question was proposed: "What then? Art thou Elias?" (John 1:21). They meant to inquire if he was literally Elijah returned again to this world, and he had no alternative but to say, "I am not" (John 1:21).

A third arrow remained in their quiver, and amid the deepening attention of the listening multitudes, they alluded to Moses' prediction that God would raise up a prophet like himself. (See Deuteronomy 18:15.) They said, "Art thou that Prophet?" and he answered, "No" (John 1:21).

They had exhausted their repertoire of questions. Their mission threatened to be fruitless unless they could extract some positive admission. "Then they said unto him, Who art thou? that we may give an answer to them that sent us. What sayest thou of thyself? He said, I am the voice of one crying in the wilderness, Make straight the way of the Lord, as said the prophet Esaias" (John 1:22-23).

How infinitely noble! How characteristic of strength! What strength and humility! When men suggested that he was the Christ, he insisted that he was only the herald of the King Himself. And when they crowded to his baptism, he reiterated that it was only the baptism of *water,* but the Christ would baptize with the *Holy Spirit* and with *fire*.

He knew his limitations! He was the greatest-born of women, yet he knew he could not say that he and God were one. He never dared to ask men to believe in himself as they believed in the Father. But there came after him One who dared to say all these things; and this is the inevitable conclusion—that Jesus was incomparably superior to the strong, Spirit-filled prophet who never wearied in declaring that an impassable chasm lay between them.

Such humility always accompanies a true vision of Christ. To the crowds, John may have seemed to fulfill all the essential conditions of the prophetic portrait of the Messiah; but although he stood on the mountain, he knew how much higher the Christ stood above him. This is apparent in his reply to the final inquiry of the Sanhedrin, "Why baptizest thou then, if thou be not the Christ, nor Elias, neither that prophet?" (John 1:25).

"John answered them, saying, I baptize with water: but there standeth one among you, whom ye know not; He it is, who coming after me is preferred before me, whose shoe's lachet I am not worthy to unloose" (John 1:26-27).

The people must have turned one to another as he spoke. What! Had the Messiah come? It could hardly be. How could He be among them and they be unaware?

But it was so, and it still is. The Christ is with us still. There may be no supernatural indications of His blessed presence as He stands in the little groups of two and three gathered in His name, but the eye of faith detects Him. He said, "He that loveth me shall be loved of my Father, and I will love him, and will manifest myself to him" (John 14:21). As the Holy Spirit revealed Him to John, He will reveal Him to us.

Six weeks passed by from that memorable vision of the opened heaven and the descending Spirit, and John had scanned the river bank to see that beautiful face again. But Jesus was in the wilderness, being tempted by the devil, for forty days and nights.

At the end of the six weeks, the interview with the delegation from the Sanhedrin took place. On the day after, when his confession of inferiority was

48

still fresh in the minds of his hearers, his eye flashed, his face lit up, and he cried, "Behold the Lamb of God, which taketh away the sin of the world. This is he of whom I said, After me cometh a man which is preferred before me: for he was before me" (John 1:29-30).

Did all eyes turn toward the Christ? Did any realize the unearthly and spiritual beauty of His presence? We know not. Scripture only tells us that on the following day, when he looked at Jesus and repeated his affirmation, "Behold the Lamb of God" (John 1:36), two disciples followed Him, never to return to their old master.

John rightly conceived of Christ's pre-existence. The phrase *"he was before me"* resembles Christ's own words: "Before Abraham was, I am" (John 8:58). John the Baptist taught his disciples that Jesus of Nazareth had a previous existence from everlasting and that He was the mighty God, the Father of the Ages, and the Prince of Peace. As for himself, he was of the earth, and of the earth he spoke. It is not surprising, therefore, that one of Jesus' disciples wrote, "In the beginning was the Word, and the Word was with God, and the Word was God. The same was in the beginning with God. All things were made by him" (John 1:1-3).

The Baptist rightly understood the sacrificial aspect of Christ's work. "Behold the Lamb of God, which taketh away the sin of the world" (John 1:29). This was breathed into his heart by the Holy Spirit.

The Jews who listened would at once connect with his words those of the law and the prophets. "The goat shall bear upon him all their iniquities unto a land not inhabited" (Leviticus 16:22). "He bare the sin of many" (Isaiah 53:12).

From the days of Abel men have brought the first-born of their flock, placed them on the altar, and consumed them with fire; but there was always a sense of *failure and insufficiency.* Priest after priest offered the lamb upon the altar, but continual repetition bore witness to the insufficiency of its atonement. "And every priest standeth daily ministering and offering oftentimes the same sacrifices, which can never take away sins" (Hebrews 10:11).

Animals at best are only symbols of the complete solution to the ever-recurring problem of human sin. From all the ages goes forth the cry, "Where is the lamb?" Then from heaven God sends forth His Son to be the answer to the universal appeal. And the heaven-sent messenger sees Jesus coming to him and cries, "Behold the Lamb of God, which taketh away the sin of the world."

He is God's Lamb. As the first Adam brought sin on the race, the second Adam has put it away by the sacrifice of Himself. Men are lost now, not because of Adam's sin or because they were born into a race of sinners, but for the sin that they *presumptuously and willfully* commit. The servant who had been forgiven by his king but took his brother by the throat brought back upon himself the full penalty. (See Matthew 18:23-35.) If any of us cling to sin, we cancel the benefits of our Savior's passion and bring back upon ourselves the penalties from which He wants to deliver us.

John understood the baptism of the Holy Spirit. "I indeed baptize you with water unto repentance: but he that cometh after me is mightier than I . . . he shall baptize you with the Holy Ghost, and with fire" (Matthew 3:11). It pleased the Father that in Jesus all the fullness of the Godhead dwelt that He might be able to communicate Him to men that were united to Him by a living faith.

The Holy Spirit is within the reach of us all, and we need to be baptized by Him, searched by His stinging flame. We need to be cleansed from dross and impurity, caught in the transfiguring energy of the Holy Spirit.

For the first time the mystery of the Holy Trinity was made manifest to man, and John understood. On one hand was the Father speaking from heaven, and on the other hand was the Spirit descending as a dove; between them was the Son of Man, who was proclaimed to be the Son of God.

The doctrine of the Holy Trinity is a profound mystery, hidden from the intellect but revealed to the humble and reverent heart. Welcome Jesus Christ as John did, and the whole wonder of the Godhead will be made known to your heart. What good is it to reason about the Trinity if you have no spiritual appetite for the gifts of the Trinity? But if you open your heart, then you will receive the gift and understand the doctrine.

John appreciated the divine Sonship of Christ. "And I saw, and bare record that this is the Son of God" (John 1:34). John knew men, knew himself, and knew Christ. He would not have said so much unless he had been profoundly convinced. The heart of the forerunner was satisfied, for he had heard the Bridegroom's voice. The Son of God had come and given John an understanding that He was true.

Chapter 9

REJOICING IN HUMILITY

From the Jordan Valley our Lord returned to Galilee and Nazareth. The marriage feast of Cana, His return to Jerusalem, the cleansing of the temple, and the interview with Nicodemus followed in rapid succession. When the crowds of Passover pilgrims dispersed, He began a missionary tour through the land of Judea. (See John 3:22; Acts 10:36-37.)

It is not likely that at first our Lord unfolded his Messianic character or taught with the same clarity as in later days. For the most part, He would adopt the cry of the Baptist. The beginning of His ministry is recorded: "Jesus came...preaching the gospel of the kingdom of God, And saying, The time is fulfilled, and the kingdom of God is at hand: repent ye, and believe the gospel" (Mark 1:14-15). But His deeds declared His royalty.

During all this time the Baptist was continuing his preparatory work in the Jordan Valley. Driven by persecution to leave the western bank for Aenon and Salim on the eastern side, a handful of followers still clung to him. "John was not yet cast into prison" (John 3:24), but the shadow of his impending fate was already gathering over him.

A Jew, probably an emissary of the Sanhedrin, brought tidings to John's disciples of the work that Jesus was doing in Judea and drew them into a discussion about the comparative value of the two baptisms. Jesus Himself did not perform the rite of baptism, but it was administered by His disciples. Therefore, it could be reported to the Baptist by his disciples, "Rabbi, he that was with thee beyond Jordan, to whom thou barest witness, behold the same baptizeth, and all men come to him" (John 3:26).

It was as though they said, "Master, is it not too bad? See how your generous testimony has been repaid! This new teacher has taken a leaf out of your program. He, too, is preaching, baptizing, and gathering a school of disciples."

But there was no tinder in John's noble breast that these sparks of hell could kindle. He had been plunged into the baptism of a holy love, which had burnt out selfishness and jealousy. Thus his reply will ever rank among the greatest utterances of mortal men. He never seemed greater as when he refused to enter into those bitter disputes and simply said, "A man can receive nothing, except it be given him from heaven" (John 3:27).

What startling differences there are among men. We are sometimes tempted to attribute their special powers and success to their circumstances, times, parents, and teachers. But there is a deeper and more satisfactory explanation. Adopting the words of the forerunner, men have nothing that they have not received from heaven, by the direct appointment and decree of God.

This is a golden sentence, indeed!—"A man can receive nothing, except it be given him from heaven." Do you have great success in your lifework? Do crowds gather around your steps and throng your auditorium? Do not attribute them to yourself. They are all the gifts of God's grace. You have nothing that you have not received. Be thankful but never vain, because He who gave may take. Great talents given imply great *responsibility* in the day of reckoning.

Use what you have. The five barley loaves and two small fishes will increase as they are distributed. (See Matthew 14:14-21.) Do not envy one more successful than yourself, or you will be convicted of murmuring against the appointment of the Lord.

Here, too, is the cure of jealousy, which more than anything else blights the soul of the servant of God. To a minister past the peak of his popularity, it is often a severe trial to see younger men stepping into positions he once held. "Why should this young man step in and take over?" Thoughts like these corrode and canker the soul. There is no stopping them unless the Spirit-energized will turns to God with the words, *"'A man can receive nothing, except it be given him from heaven.'* I will rejoice that God raises up others to do His work. I will rejoice that the Kingdom is coming, that Christ is satisfied, and that men are being saved.''

How much misery and disappointment would be saved if each of us seriously inquired what special work he was called to. Instead of being poor imitations, we would be good originals. God has meant each of us for something and equipped us with all the material necessary for its realization. We may discover it through our mental endowments, the advice of friends, the necessity of our circumstances, or the prompting of the Holy Spirit.

Every name is historic in God's estimate. The most obscure among us has his place in God's plan. ''We are his workmanship, created in Christ Jesus unto good works, which God hath before ordained that we should walk in them'' (Ephesians 2:10).

John caught sight of a fuller and richer ideal than his own. Tidings had, without doubt, been brought to him of our Lord's first miracle in Cana of Galilee. (See John 2.) How startled he must have been at the first hearing! He had announced the Lamb of God, holy and separate from sinners, but the Messiah opens His ministry among men by mingling with the simple villagers in their wedding joy, and He actually turns the water into wine! The Son of Man has come ''eating and drinking''! (See Luke 7:33-34.) Could this be He? There was no doubt that heaven had opened above Him, the Dove had descended, and God's voice had declared Him to be the ''beloved Son'' (Matthew 3:17). But what a contrast to all that he had looked for!

Further reflection, however, must have convinced the Baptist that this conception of holiness was the true one. His own type could never be universal or popular. It was not to be expected that the mass of men could spend their days in the wilderness as he had done. Consecration to God would have become synonymous with the exclusion of wife and child, home and business, and music and poetry.

But nothing that God has created is common or unclean, and all may be included within the Redeemer's Kingdom. "Every creature of God is good, and nothing to be refused, if it be received with thanksgiving: For it is sanctified by the word of God and prayer" (1 Timothy 4:4-5).

John saw that the Redeemer could not contradict the Creator and that the Kingdom was consistent with the home. This he saw, and he cried, in effect, "That village scene is the key to the Messiah's ministry to Israel. He is not only a guest at a bridegroom's table, but the Bridegroom Himself. This is my joy: *"He must increase, and I must decrease.'"*

John perceived the true nature of Christ. Consider the Baptist's creed at this point of his career. He believed in the heavenly origin and divinity of the Son of Man and the unique and divine source of His teaching. "For he whom God hath sent speaketh the words of God" (John 3:34). Knowing that human teachers could only receive the Spirit in a limited degree, he recognized that when God anointed Jesus with the Holy Spirit there was no limit—it was rich and unmeasured. John believed in Jesus' relationship to God, using the well-known Jewish phrase of *sonship* to describe His possession of the divine nature in a unique sense. And he believed that the Father had already given all things into His hand. The day was coming when He would sit on the throne of David, King of kings and Lord of lords.

To that creed the Baptist added a testimony that has been the means of light and blessing through the ages. To believe in Jesus is to have eternal life, which defies time and change. Faith is the act that opens our heart to receive the gift of God. You need only *will* to have Him, and He has already entered. To shut your heart against Him not only excludes the life which could be yours, but incurs the wrath of God. (See John 3:36.)

The only hope of a decreasing self is an increasing Christ. There is too much of the self-life in us all—chafing against God's will, refusing God's gifts, and exchanging humility and meekness for the praise of men. How can we be rid of this accursed self-consciousness and pride? We must turn our backs on our shadows and our faces toward Christ. We must look at all things from His standpoint, trying to realize how they affect Him. If we love Christ with a passion, we will think His thoughts and feel His joys.

We must view our relationship to Jesus as the marriage of our soul to our Maker and Redeemer. "Wherefore, my brethren," says the apostle, "ye also are become dead to the law by the body of Christ; that ye should be married to another, even to him who is raised from the dead, that we should bring forth fruit unto God'' (Romans 7:4).

The Son of God is not content to love us. He cannot rest until He has all our love in return: ''He looketh forth at the windows, shewing himself through the lattice.'' Our Beloved speaks, and says unto us, ''Rise up, my love, my fair one, and come away'' (Song Of Solomon 2:9-10).

Chapter 10

IN THE KING'S COURT

Our story brings us to John the Baptist's relationship with Herod Antipas, son of the great Herod, a vile prince who inherited a fourth part of his father's dominion (hence known as the Tetrarch). From an early age, he had been entrusted with despotic power and had become sensual, weak, and cruel.

All the world had flocked to see and hear John the Baptist. Every mouth was full of his peculiarities and eloquence. Marvelous stories were being told of the effect on the lives of those who had come under his influence. All this was well known to Herod. His spies were present in every great gathering, and he was well informed of all the topics that engaged the popular mind.

For some months Herod had watched the career of the preacher. When he least expected it, John was under the surveillance of the closest criticism. Herod felt that John was a just and holy man. And one day John found himself summoned to deliver his message before the court.

We may wonder why a man like Herod, who lived in a glass house, would be willing to call in so merciless a preacher of repentance as John the Baptist. His words were flung like stones, and many glass houses had crashed to the ground. But it must be remembered that most men change their tone when face to face with sinners in high places. Herod had every reason to presume that John would obey this unwritten law and refrain from anything direct and personal.

Herod knew that the land was filled with the fame of the Baptist, and it seemed an easy path to popularity to patronize the religion of the masses. He probably entertained much the same feeling toward the desert prophet that led Simon the Pharisee to invite Jesus to eat with him. (See Luke 7:36-50.)

Mark 6:20-21 suggests that the Baptist's first sermon before Herod was followed by another and another. The Baptist dealt with general subjects that were not too personal or drastic and won his genuine regard. It was a relief to Herod's mind to feel that there were many wrongs that he could set right, while the main wrong of his life was left untouched. But John knew that his duty to Herod, truth, and public morality demanded that he go further. Therefore, on one memorable occasion, he accosted the royal criminal with the crime that men were speaking of secretly everywhere and uttered the memorable sentence: "It is not lawful for thee to have thy brother's wife" (Mark 6:18).

The sermon began. As was John's custom, he attacked the sin, the formalism, and the laxity of the times. He proclaimed the advent of the Kingdom and the presence of the King. Then he demanded, in the name of God, repentance and reform. Herod was, as usual, impressed and convinced and agreed with the preacher's propositions. It was as when we watch summer-lightning playing around the horizon: we have no fear as long as it is not forked.

Presently, however, John became more personal and direct than ever before. He began to denounce the sin of men in high places. As he proceeded, a breathless silence fell on the crowd. Finally, the preacher came closer still, pointed to the princess who sat beside Herod, looked Herod in the face, and exclaimed, *"It is not lawful for thee to have thy brother's wife."*

John took the matter to the highest court. He arraigned the guilty pair before God. Laying his axe at the root of the tree—calling on Herod's conscience—he said, in effect, "I summon you before the bar of God, and your consciences bear witness against you. You know perfectly well that it is not right for you to commit adultery."

Every hearer stood aghast. A death-like hush fell on the assembly, which probably broke up in dismay. So paralyzed was everyone that no hand was laid on the preacher. We can infer that the fearless preacher simply passed out through the paralyzed and conscience-stricken crowd.

But Herodias, thirsting for John's blood, would

give her lover no rest. Perhaps one evening, when John had retired for meditation and prayer, a handful of soldiers arrested him, bound him, and led him off to the castle of Machaerus. "Herod sent forth and laid hold upon John" (Mark 6:17).

The castle of Machaerus was known as "the black tower" and lay on the east side of the Dead Sea. The ruins of the castle can still be seen on the top of a lofty hill, surrounded on three sides by unscaleable cliffs. Wild desolation reigns far and near. Here and there thick mists of steam rise, where hot sulphur gushes from clefts in the rocks.

On this impregnable site, Herod had erected a great wall with towers two hundred feet high at the corners. He built a grand palace, with halls lined with many-colored marbles, magnificent baths, and all the details of Roman luxury. Detached from the palace was a stern and gloomy prison, with underground dungeons hewn into solid rock. This was the scene of John's imprisonment.

Mark says that they *bound* the Baptist. (See Mark 6:17.) What indignation to fetter those lithe and supple limbs and place them under constraint! What a sin to bind the preacher of righteousness and imprison him in sunless vaults—what an agony! What a contrast between the happy revelry that reigned within the palace and the slow torture that the Baptist was doomed to suffer through those weary months!

Is there anything like that in your life? Outwardly

there is mirth, but inwardly there is remorse and unrest. In lonely hours a voice pierces the thickest walls of your indifference and rings into your life, where your soul seeks to close its ear in vain. It is a sad, heart-piercing cry that repeats, "It is not lawful, not lawful, not lawful." *Nothing* can stop it but repentance, confession, and restitution in the blood of Jesus Christ.

From time to time the strictness of John's imprisonment was relaxed. His disciples were permitted to see him and tell him what was happening in the world. But stranger than all was that he was summoned to have audiences with Herod himself.

As Herod thought of the manner in which the Baptist had treated him, denouncing him before his court, the fire of anger burnt fiercely within his breast. Beside him was a beautiful fiend and temptress, who knew Herod well enough to dread the uprising of his conscience at the appeals of truth. "Herodias had a quarrel against him, and would have killed him; but she could not" (Mark 6:19).

On the other side, Herod feared John, "knowing that he was a just man and an holy" (Mark 6:20). He feared the people because they held him for a prophet. And beneath all, he was afraid that God would step in and avenge any wrong done to His servant.

Between fear and anger, Herod was "much perplexed" (Mark 6:20, Revised Version). When he was with Herodias, he thought as she did and almost resolved to give the fatal order; but when he was alone, the other influence was felt, and he would send for John.

Might not Herod have attempted to induce the prophet to take back his ruthless sentence? If such an offer were made, it must have presented a strong temptation to the emaciated captive. But John had no alternative. However often the ordeal was repeated, he met the request with the same unwavering reply: "It is not lawful for thee to have thy brother's wife."

John could do nothing else. It was an act of devotion to God and His truth. He had no thought for himself and thought only of the choice and destiny of that guilty pair.

Many men are like Herod! They resemble the shallow soil on which the seed springs into rapid and unnatural growth; but rock lies close beneath the surface. First they are swayed by the voice of the preacher and moved by the pleadings of conscience, and then they feel the *fascination* of their sin and are sucked back into the sea of death.

Again and again John was ordered back to his cell. Probably twelve months passed. Each time the king failed to act on the preacher's appeals, he became harder and more liable to the sway of passion. And when a supreme moment came that he was under the influence of drink and unholy appetite, Herodias had her way, and Herod gave orders that it should be as she desired.

The story does not end here. Herod not only murdered John the Baptist but inflicted a deadly wound
on his own moral nature. The deterioration had been
so awful and complete. The love of God can say
nothing to us as long as we refuse to repent of our
sin.

Chapter 11

THE DISCIPLINE OF PATIENCE

It is touching to consider the dedication of some of John's disciples. The majority had dispersed—some to their homes and some to follow Jesus. Only a handful lingered unalienated by the storm of hate that had broken on their master. He had called them to the reality of living and had taught them to pray. He had led them to the Christ! They dared not desert him in the dark, sad days of his imprisonment and sorrow.

What a blessing to have friends who will not leave our sides when shadows darken our paths and prison wraps its chill mantle about us! To be loved like that is earth's deepest bliss!

To two of these choice and steadfast friends John confided the question that had long been forming within his soul: "And John calling unto him two of his disciples sent them to Jesus, saying, Art thou he that should come? or look we for another?" (Luke 7:19).

Can this be the man who a few months ago had

stood in his rock-hewn pulpit in radiant certainty? He had pointed to Christ and called Him the *"Lamb of God."* How great the contrast between that and his sorrowful cry, *"Art thou he?"* John the Baptist was for a brief spell under a cloud, tempted to let go of the confidence that had brought him such joy when he first saw the Spirit descending and abiding.

John was the child of the desert. The winds that swept across the waste were not freer than he. Boundless spaces had stretched above him when he slept at night or labored through the busy days. And when he found himself confined in the narrow limits of his cell, his spirits sank. He longed with the hunger of a wild thing for liberty—to move without clanking fetters, to drink of the fresh water of the Jordan, and to breathe the morning air. Is it hard to understand how his mind and spirit lost its endurance or how the depression of his physical life cast a shadow on his soul?

When first put in prison, John had expected Jesus to deliver him. Was He not the opener of prison-doors? Was not all power at His disposal? Surely He would not let His faithful follower lie in the despair of that dark dungeon!

But weeks became months, and still no help came. It was inexplicable to John's honest heart and suggested the fear that he had been mistaken after all. We can sympathize in this, for often we have counted on God to deliver us from some intolerable sorrow. But weary hours have passed without bringing Him, and we have questioned whether God were mindful of His own.

"John had heard in the prison the works of Christ" (Matthew 11:2). They were good and gentle. He had laid His hands on a few sick folk and healed them; He had gathered a number of children to His arms and blessed them; and He had spoken of rest, peace, and blessedness. John had partial views of the Christ—he thought of Him as the avenger of sin, the maker of revolution, and the judge of all. There was apparently no room in his conception for the more gentle, sweet, and tender aspect of His nature.

But isn't this what we do? We form a notion of God—partly from what we think He ought to be and partly from some notions we have derived from others—and then, when God fails to realize our conception, we begin to doubt. Like John, men form notions, founded on some faulty knowledge of Scripture, that God will act in a certain preconceived way. And when God does not fulfill *our* expectations, we say, *"Is this He?"*

Jesus turned to John's disciples and said, "Go your way, and tell John what things ye have seen and heard; how that the blind see, the lame walk, the lepers are cleansed, the deaf hear, the dead are raised, to the poor the gospel is preached. And blessed is he, whosoever shall not be offended in me" (Luke 7:22-23).

He did not say, "I am He that was to come, and there is no need to look for another." Had He done

69

so, He might have answered John's intellect, but not his heart. John might have wondered whether Christ were not Himself deceived. One question always leads to another as long as the heart is unsatisfied.

The intellect may be temporarily overpowered with the evidence, but the soul, the heart, and the spirit would miss the true knowledge that comes through purity, faith, and waiting upon God—the deepest knowledge of all. Even if one rose from the dead and came to men with the awe of the vision of the other world stamped on his face, they would not believe. (See Luke 16:31.) The evidence of the unseen and eternal must be given to the soul. The heart must be taught to wait, trust, and accept the revelations that establish the Being of God.

If Jesus healed the sick, lame, and blind and cast out demons, He could surely deliver John. It made the Baptist's heart more pensive to hear of these displays of power. John's nature was capable of yielding great results. Only three months remained of life, and in these the discipline of patience had to do its perfect work.

That is where you have made a mistake. You have thought God was hard on you but would help everybody else. You have not understood that your nature was so dear to God and so precious in His sight that He couldn't let you off lightly, give you what you wanted, and send you on your way.

We are kept waiting through the long years not because He loves us less but more. He refuses what we ask because in the long strain and tension He is making us partakers of His blessedness. John's nature would presently yield a martyr and win a martyr's crown—was not that reason enough for not giving him at once the deliverance he sought?

The Lord drew John's attention to words he seemed in danger of forgetting: "Strengthen ye the weak hands, and confirm the feeble knees. Say to them, that are of a fearful heart, Be strong, fear not: behold, your God will come with vengeance, even God with a recompense; he will come and save you. Then the eyes of the blind shall be opened, and ears of the deaf shall be unstopped. Then shall the lame man leap as an hart, and the tongue of the dumb sing: for in the wilderness shall waters break out, and streams in the desert" (Isaiah 35:3-6).

The Lord strove to convince the questioner that his views were too partial and limited and to send him back to a more comprehensive study of the Scriptures. It was as though Jesus said, "Go to your master, and tell him to take again the ancient prophecy and study it. He has taken the sterner predictions to the neglect of the gentler, softer ones. It is true that I am to come as a Mighty One, and My arm will rule for Me; but it is also true that I am to feed My flock like a Shepherd and gather the lambs in My arms."

We make the same mistake. We need to get back to the Bible and study its comprehensive words. Then we will come to understand that the present is the time of the gentler ministries. Someday He will gird on His sword and ride in a chariot of flame.

Someday He will sit upon the throne and judge those who oppress the innocent and take advantage of the poor.

"Blessed is he, whosoever shall not be offended in me" (Matthew 11:6). With these words, our Lord blessed those who have not seen and yet have believed and those who cannot understand his dealings but rest in what they know of His heart. This is the beatitude of the unoffended, those who do not stumble over the mystery of God's dealings with their life.

This blessedness is within our reach also. There are times when we are overpowered with the mystery of life and nature. The world is full of pain and sorrow, and strong hearts break under an intolerable load. God's children are sometimes the most bitterly tried. They suffer not only at the hand of man, but it *seems* as though God Himself were turned against them. The waters of a full cup are wrung out in days like these, and the cry is exhorted, "How long, O Lord, how long?"

We have the chance of inheriting a new beatitude. By refusing to bend under the mighty hand of God—questioning and murmuring—we miss the door to happiness. But if we will quiet our souls, anoint our heads, and wash our faces, light will break in on us as from the eternal morning. The peace of God will keep our hearts and minds, and we will enter on the blessedness that our Lord unfolded before the gaze of His faithful forerunner.

Chapter 12

THE LEAST IN THE KINGDOM

While John's disciples were standing there, our Lord said nothing in his praise. But as soon as they had departed, He began to speak to the multitudes about His faithful servant. It was as though He would give John no cause for pride by what He said. He desired to give His friend no additional temptation during those lonely hours.

We say our kind things before each other's faces and our hard things when their backs are turned. It is not so with Christ. Christ may never tell you how greatly He loves and values you, but while you lie there in your prison, He is saying and thinking great things about you.

Jesus chose the time that John had fallen beneath his usual level to utter his warmest and most generous words of appreciation: "Among them that are born of women there hath not risen a greater than John the Baptist" (Matthew 11:11).

The Lord judges us by what is deep within us. What are the decisions and choices of our souls?

What bud of possibility lies as yet unfurled and un-realized even by ourselves?

Jesus reckons the entire benefit of His glorious Person and work to each believer. Faith is reckoned to us for righteousness because it contains within itself the power and potency of the perfect life.

God reckoned to Abraham all that his faith was capable of producing. There is the *objective* and the *subjective*. First, through faith in Jesus, all His righteousness is accounted to us; and second, God reckons to us all the blessed fruit that our faith will be capable of when patience has done its perfect work.

Jesus drew special attention to John's independence. "What went ye out into the wilderness, for to see? A reed shaken with the wind?" (Luke 7:24). The language of the Bible is full of natural imagery, and it appeals to every age and speaks in every language of the world. If its descriptions of character had been given in the language of the philosopher or scholar, what was clear to one age would have been meaningless to the next. But the Word of God employs natural figures and parables that men can understand at a glance.

Who, for instance, has not watched the wind blowing across a marsh, compelling all the reeds to bend in the same direction? Has one resisted the current or stood forth in rebellion? Has one dared to adopt an unbending posture? Not one.

Therefore, when our Lord asked the people whether John resembled a reed shaken by the wind,

He clearly indicated one of the most prominent characteristics of John's career—his daring singularity, his independence of custom and fashion, and his determination to follow out the pattern of his own life as God revealed it to him. In John's message and demand for baptism, in his independence of the religious teachers and schools of his time, and especially in his uncompromising denunciation of Herod's sin, he proved himself to be as a deeply-rooted cedar in Lebanon and not as a reed shaken by the wind.

Christ can take the most pliant and yielding natures and make them as He made Jeremiah, "a defenced city, and an iron pillar, and brasen walls, against the whole land" (Jeremiah 1:18). He will strengthen and help you. He will uphold you with the right hand of His righteousness. Keep looking steadfastly up to Him, and He will teach your fingers to fight. You can do all things through Him that strengthens you. (See Philippians 4:13.)

A second time the Master asked the people what they went forth into the wilderness to behold. By His question Jesus implied that John was no socialite clothed in soft raiment feasting in luxury but a strong, pure soul that had learned the secret of self-denial and self-control. Too many of us are inclined to put on the soft raiment of self-indulgence and luxury. We are the slaves of fashion, perpetually considering what to eat and what to wear. We act as though life consisted in the number of things we possessed and the variety of servants that waited upon us. The exact contrary is the case! Real happiness consists not in increasing our possessions but in *limiting our wants*.

What a difference there is between making fashion our main consideration and considering first and foremost the attire of the soul in meekness, truth, purity, and unselfishness. They who set their desires upon these may be trusted to put the other in the right place.

This is the secret of making the best of your life. Discover what you can do best—the one thing that you are called to do for others, and that probably no one else can do as well. Set yourself to do this, depending on voluntary or paid helpers to do all that they can. It was in this spirit that the apostles said, "It is not reason that we should leave the word of God, and serve tables. Wherefore, brethren, look ye out among you...whom we may appoint over this business. But we will give ourselves continually to prayer, and to the ministry of the word" (Acts 6:2-4).

Jesus also drew attention to John's noble office: "But what went ye out for to see? A prophet? Yea, I say unto you, and much more than a prophet" (Luke 7:26). Nothing is more difficult than to measure men while they are living. While the fascination of their presence and the music of their voice are in the air, we tend to exaggerate their worth. But subsequent ages have only confirmed our Savior's estimate of His forerunner. To employ the words of Malachi, he was the Lord's messenger, the courier who announced the advent of the King, and the herald of that new and greater era whose gates he opened. (See Malachi 3:1.)

But our Lord went further and did not hesitate to rank John with the greatest of those born of woman. He may have had peers but no superiors. "There hath not risen a greater than John the Baptist" (Matthew 11:11).

There was a further tribute paid by our Lord to His noble servant. Two or three centuries before, Malachi had foretold that Elijah, the prophet, would be sent before the great and terrible day of the Lord came—and the Jews were always on the outlook for his coming. Even to the present day a chair is set for him at their religious feasts. Although John shrank from assuming so great a name, our Lord went beyond John's modest estimate and declared, "If ye are willing to receive it, this is Elias which was for to come" (Matthew 11:14). As He descended from the Mount of Transfiguration, He returned to the same subject: "I say unto you, That Elias is indeed come, and they have done unto him whatsoever they listed, as it is written of him" (Mark 9:13).

"But he that is least in the kingdom of God is greater than he" (Luke 7:28). John ushered in the Kingdom but was not in it. He proclaimed a condition of blessedness in which he was not permitted to have a part. And the Lord says that to be in that Kingdom gives a greatness that souls outside its boundaries cannot lay claim to.

The boy in a village school knows more on certain subjects than the greatest sages of the world.

The least instructed in the Kingdom of heaven is privileged to see and hear the things that prophets and kings longed and waited for in vain.

The character of John was strong, grand in its magnificence. He could hold fellowship with the eternal God as a man speaks with his friend and could suffer unutterable agonies in self-questioning and depression. But was this the loftiest type of character? Assuredly not; and this may have been in the Savior's mind when He made His notable reservation. To come neither eating nor drinking; to be stern, reserved, and lonely; to live apart from the homes of men; to be the severe and unflinching rebuker of other men's sins—this was not the loftiest pattern of human character.

There was something more akin to our Lord's own perfect manhood. The power to converse with God combined with the tenderness that wipes the tears of those that mourn is the pattern of the Kingdom. It is best described in those beatitudes that canonize not the stern and rugged but the tender, humble, and meek. Heaven's tenderest virtues hardly found a place in the strong and gritty character of the Baptist.

Yes, there is more to be had by the humble heart than John possessed or taught. We must wait and be still to capture the cross and shame *as well as* the throne of power. And if you are the least in the Kingdom of God, all this may be yours by the Holy Spirit, who introduces the very nature of the Son of Man into the heart that truly loves Him. ''He that is least in the kingdom of God is greater than he.''

Chapter 13

A BURNING AND SHINING LIGHT

Our Master, Christ, was on trial. He was challenged by the religious leaders because He had dared to heal a man on the Sabbath.

Our Lord was not lax in His observance of the Sabbath, but He desired to free the day from the burdens and restrictions with which the Jewish leaders had surrounded it. It was His desire to show that the Sabbath was made for deeds of mercy, goodness, and gentle kindness. The Lord Jesus was maligned and persecuted because He was the emancipator of the Sabbath from foolish and mistaken notions of sanctity.

In this case, the Lord being on trial, He proposed to call witnesses. "There was a man sent from God, whose name was John. The same came for a witness, to bear witness of the Light….He was not that Light, but was sent to bear witness of that Light" (John 1:6-8).

John "was a burning and shining lamp" (John 5:35, Revised Version). In the King James Bible, a great contrast is suggested between *lamp,* as it is given in the Revised Version, and *light.* The old version says, "He was a burning and shining *light.*" There is a considerable difference between the two. The apostle John tells us that John the Baptist "was not that Light, but was sent to bear witness of that Light."

Jesus Christ is the *Light of the World.* In every age He has been waiting to illumine the hearts and spirits of men, reminding us of the expression in the book of Proverbs, "The spirit of man is the candle of the Lord" (Proverbs 20:27).

Men are born into the world like so many unlighted candles. Jesus Christ is prepared to illuminate the spirits that are intended to be the candles of the Lord. Hundreds of professing Christians have never really been kindled. They have never been touched by the Son of God and do not know what it is to shine with His *light* and to burn with His *fire.*

What is the process of lighting? The wick of the candle is simply brought into contact with the flame, and the flame leaps to it without parting with any of its vigor or heat. It continues to burn, drawing to itself the nourishment that the candle supplies. Let Jesus Christ touch you. Believe in the Light, that you may become a child of the Light. "Awake thou that sleepest, and arise from the dead, and Christ shall give thee light" (Ephesians 5:14).

We were kindled that we might kindle others. Get light from Christ and share it. Remember that it is the glory of fire that one little candle may go on lighting hundreds of candles—one little taper may light all the lamps of a cathedral church and still not be robbed of its own glow of flame. Every Christian soul illumined by the grace of God becomes, as John the Baptist was, a lamp. Jesus is the fountain of Light, and His life is the light of men. (See John 5:26; 1:4.)

If you want to shine, you must burn. The ambition to shine is universal, but all men are not prepared to pay the price that gives the right to spread the true light of life. Famous authors and scientists spend many hours in laborious, soul-consuming toil. The great chemist will work sixteen hours a day. Such men *shine* because they *burn.*

But this is the same principle in the service of Christ. The Lord shone, and His beams have illumined multitudes of darkened souls. He suffered so He could serve. He would not save Himself because He was bent on saving others. He ascended to His throne because He did not spare Himself from the cross.

Pilate marveled that His death came so soon and sent for the centurion to make sure that in so few hours He had truly succumbed. But Pilate did not realize that in three short years He had expended His strength so fully that there was no reserve to fall back upon. There had been an inward consumption, an exhaustion of nervous power, and a wearing down of the springs of vitality. He shone because of the fire that burned within Him.

It was so with the great apostle, Paul, who gave

freely of his best. He shone because he never hesitated to burn. He affirmed that he was pressed down, perplexed, and pursued. He always bore about in his body the dying of the Lord Jesus, and the life of Jesus was manifested in his mortal flesh.

Every successful worker for God must learn that lesson. You must be prepared to suffer, for you can only help men when you die for them. If you desire to save others, then you cannot save yourself; you must be prepared to fall into the ground and die if you would not abide alone. There must be with you, as with Paul, the decaying of the outward man so that the inward man may be renewed day by day. You must be prepared to say with him, "Death worketh in us, but life in you" (2 Corinthians 4:12).

If you burn, you will shine. The burning and the shining do not always go together; often the burning goes on a long time without result. In many cases, the saints of God have burnt down to the last film of vital energy and expired, and there has been no shining that the world has taken notice of. Their bitter complaint has been, "I have labored in vain, I have spent my strength for nought, and in vain" (Isaiah 49:4). But even these will shine as the stars forever in that world where all holy and faithful souls obtain their reward.

God will provide the fuel for the burning and the shining. The fire that burned in the bush needed no fuel: "the bush was not consumed" (Exodus 3:2). With us there is a perpetual need for the nourishment of the fire of love and the light of life. The oil must be supplied to the lamp. He who has begun a good work will perform it until the day of Jesus Christ. All grace will be made to abound toward you, that you may have all sufficiency for all things and abound to every good work. (See 2 Corinthians 9:8; Philippians 1:6.)

We would have supposed that God would have placed a man like John on a pedestal or a throne so that his influence might reach as far as possible. Instead, He allowed him to spend precious months of his brief life in prison. It may be that this is your place also. It seems such a waste. Loneliness and depression are hard to endure, and the consciousness of accomplishing so little at a great cost is very painful.

But where is the lighthouse needed so much as in a dark harbor? Go on shining, and you will find some day that God will make your light stream over the world. Out of his prison cell John illuminated the age just as much as from his rock-pulpit beside the Jordan.

"Ye were willing for a season to rejoice in his light" (John 5:35). The Greek word rendered *rejoice* has in it the idea of children dancing around a torchlight as it burns lower and lower. It is as though a light were given to men for an hour to use for some high and sacred purpose; but they employ it for dancing and card-playing instead of serious tasks.

"You were willing," says Jesus, in effect, "to dance and sing in his light. As long as he spoke with you about the coming Kingdom, you listened and were glad. But when he began to call you to repentance and warn you of wrath to come, you left him."

The ministry of the gospel is but for an hour. The hourglass was turned when Jesus ascended, and it is more than likely that the last grains are running through. Take heed lest your opportunities of preparing for the serious work of life slip away unimproved and you find yourself face to face with death and judgment without hope or God.

Chapter 14

SET AT LIBERTY

Mark tells us that Herod on his birthday had a dinner for his lords, the high captains, and the chief men of Galilee. (See Mark 6:21.) Galilee was a considerable distance from the Castle of Machaerus. There would probably, therefore, have been a noble procession from Galilee to the old, grim fortress.

The days that preceded the celebration of Herod's birthday were probably filled with merry-making. Groups of nobles, knights, and ladies would gather on the terraces looking out over the Dead Sea. Picnics would be arranged into the neighboring country. Archery, jousts, and other sports would pass away the slowly-moving hours. Jests, light laughter, and buffoonery would fill the air. And all the while, in the dungeons beneath the castle, lay that mighty preacher, the confessor, forerunner, herald, and, soon to be, *the martyr*.

The Bible does not concern itself with the outward circumstances and setting of the scenes and characters it describes but with temptation, sin, and redemption, which have a meaning for us all. In this, as in every sin, three forces were at work: First, the predisposition of the soul that the Bible calls "lust" and "the desire of the mind." (See Ephesians 2:3.) Second, the suggestion of evil from without, and, finally, the act of the will by which suggestion was accepted and finally adopted.

It is in this latter phase that sin especially comes in. The essence of sin is in *the act of the will,* which allows itself to admit and entertain some foul suggestion and ultimately sends its executioner below to carry its sentence into effect.

Herod was the son of the great Herod, a murderous tyrant. Perhaps if he had come under strong, wholesome influences, he would have lived a good life. But it was his misfortune to fall under the influence of a beautiful fiend, who wrought the ruin of his soul. It is remarkable how strong an influence a beautiful and unscrupulous woman may have over a weak man. And for this reason, among others, weakness becomes wickedness. The man who allows himself to drift weakly is almost certain to discover that the strongest influences are those that result in sin.

Herod was reluctant to yield to his evil mistress. He made a slight show of resistance, as we have seen, but he did not break with her. She finally had her way and dragged him to her lowest level. Here was the cause of his ruin, as it may be of yours.

Beware of yourself. Guard against anything in your life that may open the gates of temptation. If you are weak in physical health, you guard against fatigue and impure atmospheres. How much more should you guard against the scenes and company that may wear on your soul? The Christian soldier is never off duty, never out of the enemy's reach, and never at liberty to relax his guard.

To have that banquet was the most perilous thing that Herod could have done. Lying back on his couch, lolling on his cushions, eating his rich food, quaffing the sparkling wine, and exchanging small talk with his followers, it was as though the petals of his soul were open to receive the first insidious spore of evil that floated by.

In the genesis of a sin we must give due weight to the power of the tempter, whether by his direct suggestion to the soul or by the instrumentality of men and women whom he uses for his evil purpose. In this case Satan's accomplice was Herodias—beautiful, but as deadly as a snake.

She knew the influence that John the Baptist wielded over her weak lover and that Herod attached unmeasured importance to his word. She realized that his conscience was uneasy and therefore the more liable to be affected by John's words when he reasoned of righteousness, temperance, and judgment to come. She feared that the Baptist's and Herod's consciences would make common cause against her. She was not safe as long as John the Baptist breathed. Herod feared him, and perhaps *she* feared him with more abject terror.

She watched for an opportunity, and it finally

came. The ungodly revel was at its height. The strong wines of Messina and Cyprus had already done their work. Towards the end of such a feast it was the custom for immodest women to be introduced, who, by their gestures, imitated scenes in certain well-known mythologies and inflamed the passions of the banqueters. But instead of the usual troupe, Salome, Herodias' daughter, herself came in and performed a wild dance. The girl was as shameless as her mother.

She pleased and excited Herod, who in his frenzy promised to give her whatever she might ask, even half his kingdom. She rushed back to her mother with the story of her success. "What shall I ask?" she cried.

"Ask," Herodias replied instantly, "for John the Baptist's head."

"And she came in straightway with haste unto the king, and asked, saying, I will that thou give me by and by in a charger the head of John the Baptist" (Mark 6:25).

Her mother and she were probably fearful that the king's mood would change. What was to be done must be done at once, or it might not be done at all. "Quick, quick," the girl seemed to say, "the moments seem like hours; now, in this instant, give me what I demand." The anxious demand of the girl showed how keenly she had entered into her mother's scheme.

This is how suggestions come to us, and they will come as long as we are in this world. There is a precise analogy between temptation and the microbes of disease. These are always in the air, but when we are in good health they are absolutely innocuous; our nature offers no hold or resting place for them. Temptation would have no power over us if we were in full vigor of soul. Only when the vitality of the inward man is impaired are we unable to withstand the fiery darts of the wicked one.

This shows how greatly we need to be filled with the life of the Son of God. In His life and death, our Lord vanquished the power of sin and death. The apostle John said that his converts could overcome the spirit of antichrist, because greater was He that was in them than he that was in the world. (See 1 John 4:3-4.) He who has the greatest and strongest nature within him must overcome an inferior nature; and if you have the victorious nature of the living Christ in you, you must be stronger than the nature that He bruised beneath His feet.

"The king was exceeding sorry" (Mark 6:26). The request sobered him. On one hand, his better nature revolted from the deed, and he was more than fearful of the consequences; on the other, he said to himself, "I am bound by my oath."

"And immediately the king sent an executioner, and commanded his head to be brought" (Mark 6:27).

Isn't it marvelous that a man who did not refrain from incest and murder should be so scrupulous about violating an oath that ought never to have been sworn? You have thought that you were bound to go through with your engagement because you had pledged yourself, although you know that it would condemn you to lifelong misery and disobedience to the law of Christ. But what was your state of mind when you pledged your word? Were you not under the influence of passion? Looking back on it, can't you see that you had no right to pledge half the kingdom of your nature. It is not yours to give, it is God's. And if you have pledged it through mistake, prejudice, or passion, believe that through repentance you will be absolved from your vow.

"And he went and beheaded him in the prison" (Mark 6:27). Perhaps John sent one last message to his disciples; then he bowed his head before the stroke, the body fell helpless, and the spirit was free with the freedom of the sons of God. Forerunner of the Bridegroom here, he was His forerunner there also. The Bridegroom's friend passed homeward to await the Bridegroom's coming, where he ever hears the voice he loves.

The executioner "brought his head in a charger, and gave it to the damsel: and the damsel gave it to her mother" (Mark 6:28). There would not be much talking while the tragedy was being performed. And when the soldier entered, carrying on a platter that ghastly burden, they beheld a sight that was to haunt some of them to their dying day. Often Herod would see it in his dreams and amid the light of setting suns. It would haunt him and fill his days and nights with anguish that all the witchery of Herodias could not dispel.

Months afterward, when he heard of Jesus, the conscience-stricken monarch said, "It is John whom I beheaded: he is risen from the dead" (Mark 6:16). And still afterwards, when Jesus Himself stood before him and refused to speak one word, he must have associated that silence and his deed together.

Herod's will, which had long faltered with the temptress, at last took the fatal step and executed the crime that could never be undone. If you have taken the fatal step and marred your life by some sad and disastrous sin, believe that there is forgiveness for you with God. Men may not forgive, but God will. "As far as the east is from the west, so far hath he removed our transgressions from us" (Psalm 103:12).

Chapter 15

DEATH AND RESURRECTION

John's disciples heard of his ghastly death and came to the castle to gather up his body as it lay dishonored on the ground; or perhaps they ventured into the very jaws of death to request that it might be given to them. In either case, it was a brave thing for them to do. The headless body was then buried, either in the grim hills of Moab or in a little village on the southern slopes of the Judean hills.

After performing the last rites, the disciples "went and told Jesus" (Matthew 14:12). Every mourner should go to the same gentle and tender Comforter. Go and tell Jesus! He will tell you that your brother will rise again or that your child is safe in Paradise. Every second brings you nearer to the moment of inseparable union.

There were many similarities between John's and Jesus's careers. Their births were announced, and their ministries were anticipated. Mary was unmarried, and Elisabeth was very old—an angel of the

Lord came to each. John seemed stronger and mightier, but Jesus followed close behind and took up a similar burden, pleading with the people to repent and believe the gospel.

Neither attended a prophetic school, and each avoided the great Jewish sects. They had no ecclesiastical connections and stood aloof from the Pharisees, Sadducees, Herodians, and Essenes. They attracted similar attention, gathered the same crowds, and protested against the same sins. Holding the same standard, both Jesus and John called men from formality and hypocrisy to righteousness and reality. They both received hatred from the religious leaders of their nation and suffered violent deaths. Each was loved and mourned by a handful of devoted followers.

But there the similarity ends, and the contrast begins. With John, it was the tragic close of a great and epoch-making career. When he died, men said, "Alas! a prophet's voice is silenced. What a pity that in a moment of passion the tyrant took his life! Such men are rare!"

As we turn to the death of Jesus, other feelings than those of pity or regret master us. We do not recognize that there is an end of His work but a beginning. Here at the Cross is the head of waters that will heal the nations. Here the last Adam at the tree undoes the deadly work of the first at another tree. This is no mere martyr's last agony but a sacrifice, premeditated and prearranged, that has secured the remission of sins. John's death affected no destiny but his own; the death of Jesus has affected the destiny of our race.

But there is another contrast. In the case of John, the martyr had no control on his destiny. When he opened his ministry, he had no idea that his path would end in the loneliness of a dungeon.

Jesus meant to die from the very beginning. He had received power from the Father to lay down His life. For this cause He was born, and for this He came into the world. Others die because they have been born; Jesus was born that He might die. He was never deceived about His ultimate destiny. He told Nicodemus that He must be lifted up. (See John 3:14.) He knew that as the Good Shepherd He would have to give His life for the sheep. (See John 10:11.) He assured His disciples that He would be delivered up to the chief priests and scribes, who would condemn Him to death. (See Mark 10:33.)

What answer and explanation can be given to account for the marvelous power that the Cross of Christ exerts over the hearts of men? You cannot trace it to influence or heredity, for if you preach the Cross to foreign tribes who don't have centuries of Christianity behind them the sob of the soul is still hushed. Tears of anguish are changed into tears of penitence. New hopes begin to weave the garments of a new purity. No other death effects such an immediate transformation. The death of Jesus was the supreme act of love, the gift of the

Father-heart that knew the need of the world and the only way of appeasing it.

Men have alleged that the Lord did not really rise from the dead and that the tale of His resurrection, if it were not a fabrication, was a myth. But neither of these alternatives will stand up to investigation.

When Herod heard of the works of Jesus, he said immediately, "This is John the Baptist; he is risen from the dead" (Matthew 14:2). Surely he had risen! There was a feverish dread that he would again be confronted by the murdered man, whose face haunted his dreams. Herod's followers, ready to take the monarch's cue, would be equally gullible. From one to another the rumor would pass—"John the Baptist is risen from the dead."

Why, then, did that myth not spread until it became universal? Because John the Baptist's grave disproved it. If Herod had seriously believed it or if the disciples of John attempted to spread it, it would have been easy to exhume the body and produce the ghastly evidence.

When the statement began to spread that Christ had risen from the dead, Peter and John stood up and affirmed that He was living at the right hand of God. If it had been the delusion of faithful hearts, it would have been easy for the enemies of Christianity to go to His grave and produce the body. Why did they not do it?

If it was said that it had been taken away, let this further question be answered: Who had taken it away? Not His friends, for they would have taken the wrappings with which Joseph had clothed it. Not His enemies, for they would have been glad to produce it.

It is difficult to exaggerate the significance and force of this contrast. Herod expected John to rise and gave his royal authority to the rumor of his resurrection. The disciples did not expect Jesus to rise. They held that the women were mistaken, even when the ladies assured them that it was so. But "afterward he appeared unto the eleven . . . and upbraided them with their unbelief and hardness of heart" (Mark 16:14).

After John's burial, his little band separated, never to meet in a common cause again.

When Jesus lay in His grave, this process of disintegration began at once among His followers also. The women went to embalm Him, and the men were apart. Peter and John ran together to the sepulcher, two walked to Emmaus, and Thomas was not with them when Jesus came on the evening of Easter Day.

What arrested that process? Why did the day that began with separation and decay end with a closer union than ever? Why was it that they who had been like timid deer before He died became as lions against the storm of Pharisaic hatred?

There is only one answer to these questions. The followers of Jesus were convinced that their Master was living. He was nearer to them than ever before. When the shepherd is smitten, the flock is scattered; and this flock was not scattered because the Shepherd had recovered from His mortal wound and was alive forevermore!

Surely the evidence that sufficed for them is enough for us. If they were convinced, we may be also. Let us join ourselves by faith with our Lord, certain that where He is, we too will be. In the meantime, we are assured that He is not in the grave, but risen, ascended, and glorified.

Chapter 16

A CONTINUING HARVEST

Jesus spent the last few months of His career in the tract of country beyond Jordan known as Perea. Many came to Him and went away blessed and healed. So much so that the people could not help contrasting His ministry with John's. There was a touch of criticism in their comments on the Baptist's ministry. They said, "John did no miracle" (John 10:41).

But John's whole life was a miracle—from first to last it vibrated with divine power. If he did not open the eyes of the blind, did he not cause multitudes to see themselves as sinners? Did not many a moral leper go from the waters of his baptism with new resolves and purposes to sin no more? Did not many who were buried in the graves of pride, lust, and worldliness hear his voice and come forth to life? No miracles! Surely his life was one long pathway of miracle, from the time of his birth of aged parents to the last moment of his protest against the crimes of Herod!

This is still the mistake of men. They admit that miracles may possibly have happened once, but they insist that the world has grown out of them. God, they think, is either absent or subject to His own laws!

Do not criticize the age in which we live. To look back on Pentecost with a sigh, as though there were more of the Holy Spirit or a larger presence of God in the upper room than in the room in which you sit, is a mistake. We may not have the sound of a rushing, mighty wind or the crowns of fire, but the Holy Spirit is with the Church. The atmosphere is as heavily charged with the presence and power of God as ever.

If there is any failure, *it is with ourselves*. We have not believed in the mighty power and presence of God because we have missed the outward and visible sign of His working. We have thought that He was not here because He has not been in the fire, the earthquake, or the mighty wind that rends the mountains. (See 1 King 19:11-13.) We have become so accustomed to associate the startling and spectacular with the divine that we fail to discover God in the peaceful and patient constructive forces that build up and repair the fabric of the universe.

Do not look back on the Incarnation or forward to the Second Coming as though there were more of God in either one. *God is here.* Every age is equally full of His wonder-working power.

We must not criticize the ordinary and commonplace. The pure and childlike heart will find enjoyment in *all* that God has made, although it is as familiar as a lawn sparkling with dewdrops or a stream murmuring over pebbles. A weak and unstable nature always searches for some greater sensation or some startling sign. "Show us a sign from heaven" is the incessant cry of the Pharisee and scribe. (See Matthew 16:1 and Mark 8:11.) Be content with a ministry that does not dazzle by its fireworks but sheds steady sunshine on the sacred page. If the world seems common to you, the fault lies in your eyes.

We know our limitations. We are not capable of working miracles, but we can speak true, strong words about Jesus Christ. We can bear witness to Him as the Lamb of God and urge men to repent and believe the gospel. The world would be in a sorry plight if it depended entirely on geniuses and miracle-workers. Simple, common people have laid the foundations for the superstructure of order, government, and prosperity.

Remember that God made you what you are. Be content to find out what He made you for and speak out the truth that God has revealed to you.

Nothing more deeply searches a man than the habit of speaking to people about the love of God. We cannot do it unless we are living in union with Him. It is easy to preach a sermon when you are out of fellowship with God, because you can preach your ideals or avenge on others the sins that you are guilty of. But to speak to another about Christ requires an absolutely clear sky between the speaker and the Lord.

As this practice is the most difficult, it is also the most blessed. To lead another to Jesus is to get nearer to Him. To go after one lost sheep is to share the Shepherd's joy.

The apostle Andrew seems to have dedicated his life to this. Each time he is referred to in the gospels, he is dealing with individuals. He brought his own brother to Jesus, was the the first to seek after a boy to bring to the Savior's presence, and, at the close of our Lord's ministry, he brings the seeking Greeks. Did he not learn this blessed art from his master, the Baptist?

Speak from a full heart. "We cannot but speak the things which we have seen and heard" (Acts 4:20). Does it seem difficult to always have a full heart? It is difficult, unless the secret of abiding always in the love of God and keeping the entire nature open to the Holy Spirit has been acquired. We must close our senses to the sounds and sights around us and open our souls to the unseen and eternal. We must have deep and personal fellowship with the Father and the Son by the Holy Spirit. Only then will we speak true things about Jesus Christ.

John had been dead for many months, but the stream he had set flowing continued to flow and the harvests he sowed sprang into mature and abundant fruit.

Let us live so that when we are gone our influence will linger. No one lives or dies to himself. Each grain on the ocean shore affects the position of every other. Each star is needed for the perfect balance

101

of the spheres. Each of us is affecting the lives of all that are now existing with us in the world or will exist. To untold ages, what we have been and said will affect all other beings for good or evil.

Chapter 17

THE SPIRIT AND POWER OF ELIJAH

Malachi tells us that the advent of the Messiah would be heralded by Elijah the prophet. (See Malachi 4:5.) Gabriel, four hundred years after, said that John the Baptist, whose birth he announced, would come in the spirit and power of Elijah. (See Luke 1:17.) This double prediction was referred to by our Lord when, descending from the Mount of Transfiguration, He indicated John the Baptist as the Elijah who was to come. (See Mark 9:12-13.) And, indeed, there was a marvelous similarity between these two men.

These heroic spirits were both confronted by a hostile court. In the case of Elijah, Ahab, Jezebel, and the priests of Baal withstood every step of his career; and in the case of John the Baptist, Herod, Herodias, and the whole drift of religious opinion brought him to a martyr's end.

Both Elijah and John the Baptist had the same faith in the baptism of fire. On Mount Carmel Elijah proposed the test that the God who answered by fire should be recognized as God. He erected the altar, laid the wood, placed the bull there, and drenched the altar with water; and in answer to his faith, the fire fell. (See 1 Kings 18:24-39.) John the Baptist passed through no such ordeal as that, but it was his steadfast faith that Christ would come to baptize with the Holy Spirit and fire.

Each of them turned the hearts of the people back to God. It was as though the whole nation was rushing towards the edge of a precipice that overhung a bottomless pit. It would be impossible for one man to turn back a whole army in mad flight—he would be swept away in their rush. But this is precisely what they did. Elijah turned Israel back to cry, ''Jehovah, He is God,'' and John turned the whole land back to repentance and righteousness. Publicans, soldiers, Sadducees, and Pharisees began to confess their sin, put away their evil ways, and return to the God of their fathers.

John the Baptist came in the spirit and power of Elijah—that same spirit and power are for us, too. We may be believers in Jesus, but have we received the Holy Spirit since we believed? This was the first question put by the apostle Paul when he entered the gathering of men at Ephesus. With eagerness he said, ''Have ye received the Holy Ghost since ye believed? And they said unto him, We have not so much as heard whether there be any Holy Ghost'' (Acts 19:2).

As Paul put his hand upon them, one by one, he may have said, ''This is the age of the Holy Spirit.

God Himself is prepared to anoint ordinary men for service, as He did Elijah and the Baptist. The Spirit of God is prepared to fill the human spirit so that the very power that rested on Elijah and the Baptist may rest on you also.''

The power of the Holy Spirit is for us all. He is prepared to be within us for the renewal and sanctification of character. He waits to empower us to witness for Jesus, to endure persecutions and trials—which are inevitable—and to bring other men to God. Take time to wait for the Savior, in whom the Spirit of God dwells. Ask Him to impart to you what He received on your behalf. Never rest until you are sure that the Spirit dwells in you fully and exercises through you the fullness of His gracious power. If your heart is pure, your motive is holy, and your desire is fervent, then according to your faith it has been done to you.

God is able to give us as large a portion of His Spirit as He did to the disciples on the day of Pentecost. The power of His grace has not passed away. His Kingdom is now at hand, and Christ waits to lead His Church to greater triumphs than she has ever known. Oh, that He would hasten to come forth from His royal chambers! Oh, that He would take His throne as King of kings on earth! Creation travails; the Bride and the Spirit call; the mind of man has tried all possible combinations of sovereignty, and in vain.

O Lord Jesus Christ, who at Your first coming sent Your messenger to prepare the way before You, grant that the ministers and stewards of Your mysteries may likewise so prepare and make ready Your way, by turning the hearts of the disobedient to the wisdom of the just. At Your Second Coming to judge the world, may we be found an acceptable people in Your sight. Amen.

PETER: THE DISCIPLE

Chapter 1

FIRST IMPRESSIONS THAT LAST

The contrast between God's ways and man's ways to choose and develop leaders is especially apparent in the earliest stages. *Man*, with considerable confidence in his own powers, cries: "Go to, let us build us a city and a tower whose top may reach unto heaven and let us make us a name" (Genesis 11:4). *God* begins in secret and works in the lowest parts of the earth. He calls an individual from the crowd, trains him long and patiently, and finally makes him the channel through which He pours Himself forth upon the world. Man's method often ends in a Babel of confusion, while God's will is consummated in the city of New Jerusalem which descends from above.

Peter, the leader of the apostles, was drawn from the ranks of ordinary people. His life story opens in the obscure village of Bethsaida, at the northwest corner of the Lake of Galilee. The unadorned and simple homes of the fishermen contrasted sharply with the marble palaces of the neighboring city of

Capernaum. Large numbers of Roman residents were attracted to the locality by its pleasant climate and natural beauty.

A strange anticipation and hope stirred in the hearts of many Jews that the Roman invaders would soon be driven out and the kingdom restored to Israel. Some said that the weeks of Daniel's vision had nearly expired. Others said that the aged Simeon, before his death, claimed to have held the Messiah in his arms. Some spoke of visions of angels and said that signs and voices had been attested to by credible witnesses. "The people were in expectation, and all men mused in their hearts" (Luke 3:15).

Suddenly the land was startled by the rumor that God had visited His people. A company of pilgrims, crossing the Jordan by the fords of Jericho, had encountered a strange figure who accosted them with the cry: "Repent ye: for the kingdom of heaven is at hand" (Matthew 3:2). These words gripped the national imagination and thrilled the air, already charged with electricity.

The news reached the mountain villages of Lebanon to the north and the sheepfolds of Bethlehem and Hebron to the south. It was the sabbatical year when men had plenty of leisure to leave their homes, fields, vineyards, and orchards. Streams of people poured down the Jordan Valley, eager to hear the preaching of John. Multitudes were baptized in the Jordan as they confessed their sins. Among them we may surely include the brothers Andrew and Peter, and their lifelong companions, James and John.

Peter was in the prime of his manhood. Strong, impulsive, and self-assertive, he could by no means be called a saint. Nevertheless, he was attentive to the duties and formalities of his religion, attended the temple feasts, paid his dues, and was morally respectable.

It must have seemed like the Day of Judgment when the Baptist, selecting a ledge of rock for his pulpit, stood to address the awestruck throng. John penetrated the hollow pretensions of Pharisee and scribe, comparing them to vipers. In his stern outlook, there was no hope for the sinner who refused to repent.

Peter must have been deeply moved as he listened to such preaching. Years later on the day of Pentecost, when he saw that vast crowd of Jews crying out, "What must we do?" he knew exactly the agony of their remorse. (See Acts 2:37.)

Andrew and John had already spent several hours in Jesus' holy company. They had been welcomed to His dwelling and listened with rapt attention while He spoke of heavenly things. As they listened, their hearts had burned within them. They knew, with absolute conviction, that they had found the Messiah.

Leaving Christ's presence, they said each to the other, "We must tell Simon of all this." Andrew found him and brought him to Jesus, saying, "We have found the Messiah." *They brought him,* as though it was necessary to overcome some hesitation. (See John 1:41.)

Peter was immensely impressed by that interview. This Teacher was a complete contrast to John. Those searching eyes looked into the depths of his nature, and Jesus said, "Thou shalt be called Cephas" (John 1:42).

This is how our Lord makes saints. When the heart is broken and contrite, as was the case with Peter, He speaks words of encouragement and cheer. He awakens our hope by indicating possibilities we never imagined.

At the close of that interview, Peter said to himself, "He must know how fickle and wayward I am—now hot with impulse, then cold as the snows of Lebanon. Yet if He thought me capable of becoming a rock, why should I not, with His help, become all that He wants me to be?"

Our Savior still deals with us in the same way. He tells us what we can become by the proper development of our temperament and the exercise of divine grace. As He speaks, He imparts all needed help. The stone becomes a rock, and the chief of sinners becomes the mightiest of saints. Peter's heart had opened to Christ's knock, never to close to Him again.

When he learned that Jesus was going to Galilee the next day, he resolved to accompany Him. The distance to Cana was nearly thirty miles, and the little group started on their way in the beauty of early morning. When they came within sight of the little village of Cana, Philip hurried ahead to announce their arrival to his friend Nathanael. Our Lord and

His disciples probably remained as guests in Nathanael's home.

At the marriage feast to which they were all invited on the following day, Peter and the others drank in the deepest lessons of the Master. At first Peter must have been greatly startled. Until he came under the influence of the Baptist, his highest ideal of religion had been the Pharisee with his phylacteries and the priests who officiated in the temple. Their inconsistencies enhanced the commanding splendor of the holiness of John. John was absorbed in fellowship with God, and he was absolutely fearless and unyielding. These qualities inflamed their loyalty and respect. When, therefore, John introduced them to Jesus as being incomparably greater than himself, they expected the same type of holiness in its awful, lonely splendor.

But Jesus led them to a village festival where a group of simple peasants were celebrating a wedding. He sat there among young and old, His face beaming with joy. He was welcomed by the children and greeted by the young lads and girls.

This was a new and unexpected type of holiness. What would the Baptist have done? Would he approve? But as they watched their wonderful Friend and Teacher, they became convinced that this was the religion that the world was waiting for. They could not all imitate the strict self-denial of the Baptist in the loneliness of the desert. But they could all follow in the steps of their new Master in the sweet comforts of the home.

Jesus worked His first miracle at that joyous gathering—He turned water into wine. The circumstances leading up to the miracle taught Peter several things about his new Master. Although the Lord addressed His mother with perfect respect, He was under direction from a higher source. Only a hint of a need was necessary, and He knew exactly how to meet it. Those who were called to cooperate with Him must always give Him complete obedience. (See John 2:1-11.)

These were wonderful discoveries, and it was a happy group that left Cana when the feast was over. The Passover was approaching, and they would soon leave for Jerusalem. What a story the brothers had to tell to their families!

The Master and His disciples probably traveled with their own families to the feast, but they met again in Jerusalem. Peter and the rest watched with wonder as their gentle Master cleansed the temple as though girded with power like Elijah. They pondered His affirmation that He would rebuild the temple in three days. Not until He was risen from the dead did they understand His meaning.

Nine months were spent traveling with Jesus throughout Judea. Peter may have paid occasional brief visits home, but he returned to assist the Master in baptizing those who confessed and forsook their sins. "Though Jesus himself baptized not, but his disciples" (John 4:2). To avoid the increasing suspicion of the Pharisees, the Lord and His disciples returned through Sychar and Samaria to Cana, where apparently the group disbanded temporarily. Jesus returned to Nazareth, and the disciples returned to their homes.

For a period of nine months, our Lord seems to have ministered without the disciples. He probably was in touch with them, but they were not openly associated with Him. He was quietly preparing them for the great future which was as yet veiled from view. He went alone throughout all Galilee, "teaching in their synagogues, and preaching the gospel of the kingdom, and healing all manner of sickness and all manner of disease among the people; And his fame went throughout all Syria....and there followed him great multitudes of people from Galilee, and from Decapolis, and from Jerusalem, and from Judaea, and from beyond Jordan" (Matthew 4:23-25).

Chapter 2

A FISHER OF MEN

Peter and John had been friends from boyhood and were partners in the fishing business. They were committed disciples and friends of Him who was moving the whole country. Jesus' life, deeds, and words were always on their lips as they floated over the lake together. Probably they had been speaking of Him as they drew to shore after a night of fruit-less toil, wondering if they would see Him soon.

They disembarked and were rinsing out their nets when they became aware of the approach of a vast crowd. In the midst of the throng, they caught a glimpse of their beloved Teacher and Friend. Ins-tantly they forgot their weariness and disappoint-ment. Jesus came to Peter's boat and asked that it be anchored within one of the rock-lined inlets that indented the shore. There He sat and spoke to His congregation.

When our Lord prepares a vessel for His use, He has to establish His absolute authority and right to command. There can be no argument, hesitancy, or holding back. Spirit, soul, and body must be absolutely submitted to Him, at whatever cost. Peter and the others were prepared to give Him their loyal allegiance in the realms of morals and duty. But they were startled when, invading their own area of expertise, Jesus said to Peter, "Launch out into the deep, and let down your nets for a draught" (Luke 5:4). For a moment Peter's obedience faltered, and he replied, "Master, we have toiled all the night, and have taken nothing" (Luke 5:5).

Peter was prepared to obey the slightest precept that came from the Master's lips. But how could one who had spent His days in the carpenter's workshop take command of a boat and direct the casting of a net? Morning was no time for fishing. The glare of light revealed the meshes of the nets, and the fish were now in the shallower part of the lake. The other fishermen that might see his boat leaving shore at such an hour, evidently prepared for fishing, would laugh and say he was crazy.

The same thing happens with all who have been greatly used by Christ. Often long after we have become disciples, the Master comes on board the ship of our life and assumes supreme control. For a moment or an hour there may be question and hesitation. We are used to making our own plans and following our own course. Dare we hand over the entire command to Christ? We are blessed if, after such a moment of hesitation, we reply: "Nevertheless at thy word I will put out even to the deep, and let down the nets for a draught" (Luke 5:5).

You can never depend on Christ's co-partnership and blessing unless you are prepared to sail under His orders and fulfill His commandments, obeying the voice of His Word. Jesus has a place and a use for you, but you must surrender yourself to Him. Refuse to be bound by customs and circumstances. Make Christ your Captain, while you take the oars!

To Peter's surprise, the boat passed over many well-known fishing grounds before our Lord told them to let down the nets. Immediately all hands set to work. The necessary preparations were hardly completed when it was evident that they had netted so many fish that the nets were strained to the breaking point. Peter's boat was lurching dangerously, and he called for his partners. They came and filled both of the boats, so that the gunwales were almost level with the water. Peter realized for the first time what partnership with Christ means and how absolute obedience on our part secures absolute cooperation on His.

What a lesson is here for us all! All we have to do is have washed and mended nets, trust the Master to show us where the fish are, and believe that He will do the rest.

On the day of Pentecost, Peter again let down his net, this time into the vast crowds. Again the Lord repeated the miracle of the Galilean lake and filled his net with three thousand souls. In the house of Cornelius, his net had hardly touched the water when the catch filled it. "As I began to speak, the Holy Ghost fell" (Acts 11:15). On each occasion Peter must have looked into the face of Jesus with a happy smile and said, "Ah! Lord, here is the Lake of Galilee over again."

The Master revealed His purpose for His disciples when they had again beached their boats: "Come ye after me, and I will make you to become fishers of men" (Mark 1:17). Earnest believers linger wistfully over these words, longing to extract from them the precious secret of successful soul-winning. Many godly ministers with a carefully organized church, surrounded by devoted people, have watched, almost enviously, the success of some simple evangelist who lifts netfuls of fish from the great depths of human life into his boat.

One expert fisherman advises: "Keep yourself out of sight." Another claims that the bait and method must be carefully adapted to the habits of the fish. A third insists on patience. All suggestions are good, but the study of this narrative may bring us further into the heart of the matter and the mind of our Lord.

Successful soul-winning is based on the consciousness of personal sinfulness. The untiring labors of the apostle Paul laid the foundations of the Gentile Church. But as he reviews the past and considers his natural condition, he does not hesitate to speak of himself as the chief of sinners and the least of saints. (See 1 Timothy 1:15 and Ephesians 3:8.)

The ringleaders in the devil's army make great soldiers for Christ. Their knowledge of Satan's strategy is invaluable. The sinner knows the bitterness of the wages of sin, as an unfallen angel or an innocent child cannot. They have infinite patience because the Lord had patience with them. They bear gently with the hard-hearted and with those who resent their approach because they have experienced the same doubts and fears.

Peter and the rest had known the Lord for at least eighteen months, but they were unaware of His true majesty and glory. To them He was the carpenter of Nazareth, a holy man, a marvelous teacher, and a wonder-worker. It never occurred to them that they were in daily touch with the Lamb of God or that He had emptied Himself and assumed the role of a servant for them.

But as Peter felt the tug and pull of the bursting net, he realized that his Teacher and Friend must have power which no mortal could wield. He was in God's presence, and he had not known it. At once, the sinfulness of his own heart was laid bare, and he cried, "Depart from me; for I am a sinful man, O Lord" (Luke 5:8). Immediately Jesus said, "Fear not; from henceforth thou shalt catch men" (Luke 5:10).

Expect to hear the Lord answer your confession of sin with a new summons to take your boat and get ready for a blessing. This experience will happen many times as we approach the summit of our Lord's pure holiness.

We may detect the presence of sin and evil in actions and attitudes which once seemed harmless and innocent. The true Christian knows that his own righteousness is as filthy rags and confesses that he is far from perfect. He learns to say with the apostle Paul, "This one thing I do, forgetting those things which are behind, and reaching forth unto those things which are before, I press toward the mark for the prize of the high calling of God in Christ Jesus" (Philippians 3:13-14).

Failure and sin do not necessarily exclude anyone from divine partnership in soul-winning. "Depart from me," cried the conscience-stricken disciple. It was as though he said, "I will bring You, Lord, to the spot where I took You on board this morning. Then You must go Your way and I will go mine. I will always love You, but I am not good enough to remain with You." Under his breath he may have whispered to himself, "But I do not know how I can live without You."

Our Lord assures us that when sin is repented of and confessed, it need not remove us from His presence or service. He can work with sinful men who are conscious of their sinful nature. No sin is too great for Him to deal with or too foul for Him to cleanse. Stay with Jesus. He will cleanse, heal, and save you and then use you to save thousands of sinners like you.

Soul-winning, to be successful, must be the absorbing purpose of our lives. It cannot be one interest among many. The disciples left everything and followed Jesus. We can imagine that after this moving exchange of words, Peter returned home to think over the amazing life that now opened before him.

The fire burned in his heart. What else was worth living for? Surely he must obey the call, "Come, follow Me!"

We cannot suppose that Peter immediately felt the Master's love for the souls of men. That was acquired later. In the beginning, he was content to follow Him, listen to His words, and be His companion and helper. But soon he and his companions began to be filled with the same passion, until it became the reason for their existence.

It will be the same with us. As we walk with Christ, by the constant aid of the Holy Spirit, we will be conformed to His image. His thoughts and yearnings will be ours, and we will long to see Him honored, loved, and exalted. We will become identified with His interests, without a backward look on ourselves. May we become partners with Christ in His great passion for the salvation of men!

Chapter 3

PREPARING FOR SERVICE

The first lesson Jesus taught His disciples was that their association with Him would inevitably involve them in spiritual warfare. On the first Sabbath after their decision to follow Jesus, the little group of fishermen accompanied Him to the usual synagogue service. When the customary exercises were concluded, their Leader and Friend was invited to address the congregation. With words of spirit and life, He unfolded the mysteries of the Kingdom. The sharp contrast between His address and the dull deliverances of the scribes to which the people were accustomed struck them with astonishment. "He taught them as one that had authority" (Mark 1:22).

The hush of the enthralled assembly was suddenly broken by the cry of a man's voice. "Let us alone," was the demand. "What have we to do with thee, thou Jesus of Nazareth?...I know thee who thou art, the Holy One of God" (Mark 1:24).

The disturbance caused by that wailing cry from the abyss must have been very startling. Peter suddenly realized that his Master's holy character must discover, arouse, and call into hostility the whole kingdom of evil spirits. The warfare he had enlisted in was not against flesh and blood but against the wicked spirits that rule the darkness of this world. When Jesus commanded the unclean spirit to be silent and come out of this tormented person, it had to obey. The disciples shared in the amazement of the crowd, but they saw clearly that the weapons of their warfare would have to be spiritual to pull down satanic strongholds.

The scene in that synagogue caused Peter to realize that a vast underworld of evil spirits would be violently perturbed at any attempt to rescue their victims. Their one delight was to deceive and torture men, but they could not withstand the power of God.

Peter could easily understand the effect produced on them by the Lord's purity. He also had cried, "Depart from me; for I am a sinful man, O Lord" (Luke 5:8). But all his fear passed since he yielded his will to submit to Christ's undisputed authority. The presence of Jesus for him now meant joy unspeakable and full of glory. He was prepared to hear the Master say, "Heal the sick, cleanse the lepers, raise the dead, cast out devils" (Matthew 10:8). "Behold, I give unto you power to tread on serpents and scorpions, and over all the power of the enemy: and nothing shall by any means hurt you" (Luke 10:19).

The second lesson was the need for gentleness in

ministry. Peter was a strong man with a loud voice. He required a considerable amount of training before he could speak, as he does in his epistles, with compassion and courtesy. The tough fisherman became clothed with that "meek and quiet spirit, which is in the sight of God of great price" (1 Peter 3:4). The first lesson in this quality was given in his own home.

After the amazing deliverance witnessed in the synagogue, the Lord accepted the invitation of Peter and Andrew to come home for rest and refreshment. James and John were included in the invitation. But when the guests reached the door of the fisherman's home, Peter's wife took him aside and hurriedly whispered that her mother was ill with a dangerously high fever.

Luke says that "they besought him for her" (Luke 4:38). In addition to the marvel of her immediate recovery, they wondered at the tender gentleness with which the Master took her by the hand and raised her up. Peter had no idea that in a few years he would do the same for a lame man on the temple steps and for the beloved Dorcas at Joppa.

The world needs tenderness as well as strength. Strength is never perfected until it is tender. The danger of modern charity is that it does everything in precise and strict adherence to a prescribed code, leaving no room for the spontaneous workings of Christlike tenderness. Lives are blighted, homes are wrecked, and bright young hopes withered, for lack of tenderness.

The third lesson was a glimpse into the anguish of the world. Nothing less could sustain the disciples, especially Peter, in all future trials and disappointments. That evening, all that were diseased and possessed, together with their agonized friends, gathered in the street where Peter lived. He could not have believed that such misery and pain was concealed near his home. They came for a touch from the Master. As Peter looked into their tormented faces, the compassion that comes from God began to grow in his heart. Filled with wonder, he watched Jesus patiently minister to one after another. Whether it was a single leper or a crowd, Jesus was always moved with compassion in the presence of human need.

Cold hearts are not used by God to win lost souls. He preaches best who loves most. If we are content to labor without seeing results, we need not expect any. But if our soul breaks with longing, the answer will not delay. "Blessed are they which do hunger and thirst after righteousness: for they shall be filled" (Matthew 5:6).

The fourth lesson revealed the source of the Master's power. In the early morning, Peter's household sought for their beloved and honored guest. He had risen a great while before day and departed into a solitary place where He prayed. Jesus could cast out demons and heal a crowd of sick people, but He was conscious of the expenditure of spiritual force. He knew "that virtue had gone out of him" (Mark 5:30). Jesus needed to pray. Peter never forgot his Master's prayer habit, and he followed in those blessed footsteps.

John Wesley told his preachers, "Why are we not more holy? Why do we not live for eternity and walk with God all day long? Do we rise at four or five in the morning to be alone with God? Do we observe the five o'clock hour for prayer at the close of the day? Let us fulfill our ministry."

God's power is available to anyone who is wise and humble enough to study and obey the necessary conditions of its operation. The poor, the weak, and the despised of this world can enjoy great manifestations of divine energy equally with the cultured and refined. People with simple faith and childlike dispositions can be greatly used by God because they are humble and helpless in their own estimation.

The conditions on which spiritual power operates are clearly set forth in the threefold temptation through which our Lord passed at the beginning of His public ministry. (See Matthew 4:1-11.)

We must refuse to employ divine power for selfish uses. Then we will be trusted with it on behalf of others, and God will meet our needs. True victory is won, not by conflict or force, but by service, sacrifice, and suffering. Divine power is granted only for the help and blessing of others. It should never lift us up in pride.

When the apostles returned from their first preaching tour, they excitedly told Jesus about the things they had done and taught. They needed an opportunity to discuss their recent experiences, receive guidance on their difficulties, and share their joys. "And he said unto them, Come ye yourselves apart into a desert place, and rest a while: for there were many coming and going, and they had no leisure so much as to eat" (Mark 6:31).

The people, however, had noticed the course taken by the boat as the weary apostles departed. The crowd rushed around the lake and expectantly waited for Christ. Immediately, our Lord put all other considerations aside to minister to more than ten thousand people. "He was moved with compassion toward them, because they were as sheep not having a shepherd: and he began to teach them many things" (Mark 6:34).

But the most astounding event happened at the end of the day. With five loaves and two small fish, Jesus fed the vast crowd. "They did all eat, and were filled. And they took up twelve baskets full of the fragments, and of the fishes" (Mark 6:42-43).

Peter and the rest of the apostles never forgot that experience. They saw the extraordinary contrast between their Master's simple lifestyle and His hospitality. They had heard about His forty-day fast when He was tempted to use His power to turn the stones of the desert into bread. Why had He not used it for His own need? Why had He not given them a banquet every day?

God will trust no one with His power who will use it for his own satisfaction and indulgence. We are tested in the wilderness by lonely hours and by long abstinence from the things that others crave and enjoy. Only when we have passed the test does God allow us to make full use of that power for the salvation and enrichment of others.

This is the reason for the wilderness experience. Is God angry with you? No! Has He forgotten to be gracious? No! He is testing you before He entrusts you with His power.

After the meal, the crowd was filled with a sudden impulse to make Jesus their leader in a revolt against their Roman oppressors. But Jesus would have none of it. He had already fought this battle out in the wilderness when the devil offered Him the kingdoms of the world. He knew that this world could become His only through His death on Calvary.

What significance this lesson has for us all! Not by might or by power will the Church win her victory but by service, suffering, and the sacrifice of tears and blood. Only in this way does the Kingdom come.

After sending the crowds home and spending time alone in prayer, Jesus set out to meet His disciples. "He cometh unto them, walking upon the sea" (Luke 6:48). He used the water as the pavement of His approach. Often the storms teach us to appreciate the wonderful resources of His nature. When we follow the path He has clearly indicated, the difficulties we encounter do not prove that we are wrong but only that He has some fresh revelation to make of Himself. We can absolutely trust our Lord to take all the risks involved in our obedience to His will.

Peter was filled with a spirit of adventure. He felt that this occasion called for a startling manifestation of love and faith and a display of his splendid courage. He may have been unaware of the pride that prompted his actions. When Peter asked to be commanded to come to Jesus on the water, our Lord simply invited him to step out. Peter did, but his faith was imperfect, and he began to sink.

Although he was a good swimmer, Peter cried for help. Immediately the Lord caught him, and they went together to the boat. No rebuke fell from those wise and gentle lips except the question, "Wherefore didst thou doubt?" (Matthew 14:31). Obviously, one reason for Peter's failure was that he watched the wind and waves rather than the face of his Lord. But there was a deeper reason for the failure. His faith was imperfect.

If you cannot take hold of God's promises for the step you are making, it is likely to fail because pride, boastfulness, or selfishness is deteriorating your spiritual life. Get rid of it by setting your mind on the cross. Crucify your flesh with its weak affections and strong desires. Speak boldly what our Lord said under similar circumstances: "Get thee behind me, Satan: for thou savourest not the things of God, but the things that be of men" (Mark 8:33).

Peter learned his lesson well. With the undying impression of that hour, he later wrote, "Humble yourselves therefore under the mighty hand of God, that he may exalt you in due time" (1 Peter 5:6).

Chapter 4

BUILDING THE KINGDOM

A crisis was upon Jesus. He was surrounded by a crowd who only desired to live on His bounty and make Him the tool of their political party. When Jesus made it clear that His mission was not to give food and drink but to preach the gospel of the Kingdom, many of those who had vowed their allegiance renounced Him and quietly withdrew. The synagogue where He taught was emptied, except for the little group of apostles who had witnessed the shattering of their Master's popularity along with their private ambitions.

He looked at them and asked, "Will ye also go away?" (John 6:67). Peter's reply came without hesitation: "Lord, to whom shall we go? thou hast the words of eternal life. And we believe and are sure that thou art that Christ, the Son of the living God" (John 6:68).

Men have tried every system of government, every phase of philosophy, and every form of religious cult. Suicide is on the increase. Immorality and divorce suggest the decay of love, hope, and faith. Ancient landmarks are swallowed by the advancing tides of change. This is the predicted hour of trial—"which shall come upon all the world, to try them that dwell upon the earth" (Revelation 3:10). To whom shall we go?

Shall we go to the skeptic? He will ridicule our longings as the fantasies of disordered minds. It is as though one were to assure a hungry man that the feeling of hunger was simply imagined.

Shall we go to the religious man? He will offer us ceremonies fragrant with all that satisfies our sense of beauty and gratifies our reverence for tradition. But these are inadequate to quench the soul's longing for the living God.

Shall we go to the religions of the East? Does Confucius, Buddha, or Mohammed have the medicine that can bring forgiveness and peace with God?

Every door opens on despair. There is no satisfaction except in Christ. Jesus said, "I thank thee, O Father, Lord of heaven and earth, because thou hast hid these things from the wise and prudent, and hast revealed them unto babes. Even so, Father: for so it seemed good in thy sight" (Matthew 11:25-26).

Jesus' teachings are directly opposed to the tendencies of human nature. They opposed Jewish exclusiveness on the one hand and Gentile culture on the other. But He never tried to gain followers by lowering His standards. He made no concessions to the passions or prejudices of His hearers. Although His human nature craved for fellowship and faith,

He stood as a rock in unwavering steadfastness to His great ideals.

The mystery in Jesus' words repels the superficial, but that same mystery is an additional reason for our faith. People go away because they do not understand. But a Christ whom we could completely understand and analyze would be no Christ for us. We desire joy unspeakable, peace that passes understanding, and love that passes knowledge; and we find Jesus always before us.

Jesus satisfies. He does more for us than we can ask or think. "Eye hath not seen, nor ear heard, neither have entered into the heart of man, the things which God hath prepared for them that love him" (1 Corinthians 2:9).

For two and a half years our Lord had lived among His apostles. Only six months of education remained before He was taken from them. During this period, His teaching became much more intense.

He began by asking the searching question, "Whom do men say that I the Son of man am?" (Matthew 16:13). It was universally acknowledged that He was no ordinary man. People felt that a divine fire was burning within Him. Some expressed the belief that the Baptist had risen from the grave. Others said that Elijah, whom Malachi had taught them to expect, had come to them. Others traced a resemblance between Jesus and one of the old prophets.

Our Lord was not disappointed or surprised by these replies. It mattered little what conclusions had been reached in the court of public opinion. These inquiries were only intended to lead up to the second and all-important question: "But whom say ye that I am?" (Matthew 16:15).

Jesus waited expectantly for the reply. It came instantly and decisively from the lips of Peter, always the spokesman for the rest: "Thou art the Christ, the Son of the living God" (Matthew 16:16). The fisherman had been taught the mystery never before revealed to men.

Jesus said to Peter, "Blessed art thou, Simon Barjona: for flesh and blood hath not revealed it unto thee, but my Father which is in heaven. And I say also unto thee, That thou art Peter, and upon this rock I will build my church; and the gates of hell shall not prevail against it" (Matthew 16:17-18).

For the first time, our Lord spoke of His Church. Until now, the Church existed only in the councils of eternity. It was destined to be His bride, His body, and His fulfillment. Through it, He could manifest the complete glory of His nature.

"My church!" From eternity Christ loved her. By His blood He redeemed her. Through His Spirit and by His Word, He is cleansing her. One day He will present to Himself "a glorious church, not having spot, or wrinkle, or any such thing" (Ephesians 5:27). The Holy Spirit is completing the Church in these last days and preparing her to be forever with the Lord.

The Church is the special object of hatred to the dark underworld of fallen spirits, which our Lord refers to as "the gates of hell." Jesus clearly anticipated the long and weary opposition that would be directed against His Church. The Church can only overcome "by the blood of the Lamb, and by the word of their testimony" (Revelation 12:11).

The secret of the Church's victory over her foes consists in her foundation doctrine. The Church was not founded on an impulsive and fallible man, who later received the sharpest rebuke ever given by Jesus. Rather, the Church's foundation is the *revelation* of our Lord as "the Son of the living God."

The Greek phrasing of our Lord's reply leaves no doubt as to His meaning. *Petros,* Simon's new name, means a stone or a bit of rock, broken from its parent bed. *Petra* refers to the rock-bed itself. Our Lord carefully makes the distinction. If He had intended Peter to be the foundation of the Church, He would have said, "Thou art Peter, and on *thee* I will build My Church." But carefully selecting His words, He said, "Thou art Peter, a stone, a fragment of rock. Under the power of God's Spirit you have spoken with strength and certainty; but I cannot build on you. I must turn from Petros to Petra, from a fragment to the great truth, which for the moment has inspired you. The truth of My eternal relationship to the Father is the *only* foundation. Against this foundation, the waves of demonic and human hatred will break in vain."

Jesus then promised, "And I will give unto thee the keys of the kingdom of heaven: and whatsoever thou shalt bind on earth shall be bound in heaven:

and whatsoever thou shalt loose on earth shall be loosed in heaven'' (Matthew 16:19).

This is the secret of the blessed life. Go through the world opening prison-doors, lifting heavy burdens, and giving light, joy, and peace to the oppressed.

Chapter 5

A TASTE OF DIVINE GLORY

On the last day of our Lord's visit to Caesarea
Philippi, He asked His closest three apostles to accompany Him for a time of rest and prayer on the
upper slopes of Mount Hermon. Little realizing what
awaited them, they accompanied Him to a scene
which left an everlasting impression. While Jesus
prayed, Peter and the others became eyewitnesses
of Christ's majesty as He was transfigured before
them. Glory streamed through His garments. His
clothing became whiter than snow with the glory
of the Only-begotten of the Father.

The appearance of Moses and Elijah added to the
magnificence of the spectacle. Moses was the embodi-
ment of the Law, and Elijah represented the Prophets.
In both cases, the circumstances of their removal
from earth had been remarkable. Moses died on the
lonely heights of Mount Pisgah and was buried by
God in an unknown grave. Elijah had gone home in
a chariot of fire. They came now to offer special encouragement to the Redeemer at this time of crisis.

Only a few days before, our Lord had foretold His death. Immediately Peter, speaking for the rest, had sought to dissuade Him. "This will never happen to You!" Love and passionate devotion inspired this impulsive soul to chastise his Lord. (See Matthew 16:22.)

"Get thee behind me, Satan," must have been a startling rebuke to Peter and his companions. To them, the death of the cross seemed as unthinkable as it appeared unnecessary. Certainly He who had saved others could save Himself from such incredible shame and torture! Their Lord might have incurred the hatred of their religious leaders, but any conflict between Him and the Roman authorities, who alone could impose death by crucifixion, was unnecessary.

But now, to their surprise, they discovered that heaven could speak of nothing else! In Moses and Elijah, redeemed humanity furnished two of its strongest and noblest ambassadors to reinforce and strengthen our Lord before He went to Jerusalem to die. He was fulfilling the plan made before the foundation of the world. Moses and Elijah, as the chosen emmissaries of the eternal world, assured Him of the Father's help and of the glory waiting when the bitterness of death had passed.

Moses would speak of the Passover lamb which was slain before the Exodus when his people were set free. Elijah would remind Him that it was written in the Prophets and the Psalms that the Christ should suffer and enter into glory.

Peter made a suggestion which was as foolish as it was hasty. He later admitted that he did not know what he was saying. The crucifixion would have been impossible if our Lord had disregarded the cries of a lost world and spent His remaining years in a tabernacle on the mountain. Peter wanted Moses and Elijah to be detained from their blessed residence and ministry in heaven.

As he spoke, he and his fellow apostles watched a cloud descend which enveloped the radiant vision. It was no ordinary cloud but probably the Shekinah-cloud that filled Solomon's temple on its dedication. From it, the voice of God was heard bearing witness to the Savior as the beloved Son and demanding homage from all. Jesus turned His back on Paradise for Himself so that He might open Paradise for the dying thief on the cross and for us.

When the cloud had passed, He was left alone with His apostles. Together they took the road to Jerusalem and to Calvary. Peter's home in Capernaum provided a convenient place to stop on the way. But things had changed dramatically since the earlier days of Jesus' ministry. The streets were no longer crowded by the sick waiting for His healing touch, and the synagogue was not open to His teaching. The seeds of jealousy and suspicion that the Pharisees had sown with lavish eagerness had produced a harvest of mistrust and hatred.

One symptom of this changed attitude presented itself almost immediately upon His arrival. The collectors of the temple tax encountered Peter with the challenge, "Doth not your master pay tribute?" (Matthew 17:24). This tax supplied the funds for the maintenance of the temple. It was a voluntary tax, but religious teachers, such as rabbis, were exempted from payment. The demand from the collectors proved that the respect and reverence which had formerly surrounded Jesus had broken down.

When Peter reached home, Jesus anticipated his story by asking whether it was customary for kings to demand tribute from their sons. Our Lord had noticed the change in the treatment He might henceforth expect. His opponents would use a refusal of payment as another reason for denouncing Him and His teaching before the people. Therefore, Jesus declared that He was willing to meet the demand for both Himself and Peter.

When questions arise in life which do not involve principle and conscience, we should be prepared to make concessions to the customs of those whom we may be able to influence for good. The apostle Paul said that all things were lawful to him, but they might become a stumbling block to others. "Give none offence, neither to Jews, nor to Gentiles, nor to the church of God: Even as I pleased all men in all things, not seeking mine own profit, but the profit of many, that they may be saved" (1 Corinthians 10:32-33).

The Master probably arranged that a certain amount of money be allocated from the common purse for the maintenance of Peter's home and family. When you give yourself completely to Christ and

His service, not at your whim but by His direct invitation, you may depend on His provision. Even if your faith fails, He will remain faithful.

Before you call, He will answer. He knows that you have given up many things for His sake that others take for granted. They have not been called to your life of consecration and self-denial. For Christ's sake, you have renounced sources of income about which other Christians have no scruples. For the gospel's sake you have renounced a love that, however pure in itself, refused to go all out for God. For the sake of dying multitudes in far-off lands, you are breaking away from old moorings and launching out into untried seas. Be of good cheer! Your Master knows your situation. Do not hesitate to take your need to Him. He promised, "Every one that hath forsaken houses, or brethren, or sisters, or father, or mother, or wife, or children, or lands, for my name's sake, shall receive an hundredfold, and shall inherit everlasting life" (Matthew 19:29).

The fish Peter caught that afternoon yielded one coin—the stater—which paid the tax for Jesus and Peter. Jesus links Himself to a sinful man. Who can separate what God has joined together? Life, death, things present, or things to come can never snap that bond.

"Take, and give unto them for me and thee" (Matthew 17:27). Jesus has received gifts for us and yearns to bestow them; but He requires people to distribute to the crowd, just as His apostles took the bread and fish from His hands and gave to the five thousand.

This is the law of Christ's own life. Having received the Father's promise of the Holy Spirit, He sent Him to the waiting Church. Our Lord has received His inheritance from the Father and has given it all away to us, as co-heirs with Himself. He has taken and given.

The tragic failure of innumerable multitudes is that they have not learned to take. They pray fervently, but they have not acquired the art of receiving. Our Lord said, "What things soever ye desire, when ye pray, believe that ye receive them, and ye shall have them" (Mark 11:24).

We pray, agonize, and strive, but we often fail to see that the cargo has already been delivered on the wharf and is waiting to be claimed and taken away. Before we can take, we must be sure that we are not prompted by personal ambition but are acting in the name and according to the nature of our Lord. When these conditions are fulfilled, we hear our Father say, "Child, you are always with Me, and all that I have is yours. Take, and go on your way to give."

We may not *feel* that we have received. We base our faith on the unfailing faithfulness of God. We go forth to act on the assurance that we have received ample and inexhaustible supplies. Whatever demands knock at our door, our Master will meet them all.

We cannot give unless we have learned to take; and we cannot take unless we are prepared to give. Let us go forth. Aching hearts, marred lives, and out-

142

stretched hands are on all sides. Let us be channels through which God may answer prayers. "Give, and it shall be given unto you; good measure, pressed down, and shaken together, and running over, shall men give into your bosom. For with the same measure that ye mete withal it shall be measured to you again" (Luke 6:38).

Chapter 6

MOLDING THE CHARACTER OF DISCIPLES

We must never forget that our Lord dealt with His apostles as individuals. He studied their idiosyncrasies and administered special correction or instruction as each required. Each member of that inner circle had strong personal characteristics which had to be trained before they were prepared for the special work that awaited them as foundation stones in the New Jerusalem.

Judas and Peter seemed to give Jesus the most concern. Judas because his nature was secretive and subtle, and Peter because his fervid and impulsive temperament was constantly pushing him into extreme positions from which he needed to be rescued. At one moment, he said to Jesus, "Depart from me"; at the next, he left all to follow Him. He won the high commendation, "Blessed art thou"; and then he is addressed as Satan. Within a single hour he is ready to fight for the Master, and then he denies that he had ever known Him.

Teaching Peter to have stability of character and

144

enabling him to lead the Church in its conflict with the world presented a serious problem to his Master and Friend. Jesus never doubted the sincerity of Peter's affection, but He was sorely tried by its impulsive exhibitions.

Although Peter is not specifically mentioned, he probably took a prominent part in the hot disputes which broke out from time to time among the disciples. When our Lord reached Capernaum after returning from Mount Hermon, He entered Peter's house and asked them, "What was it that ye disputed among yourselves by the way?" (Mark 9:33). An uncomfortable silence settled over the group because they had disputed among themselves who was the greatest. Jesus sat down, called them around Him, and told them that the only way for a man to become first in His Kingdom is by being last of all and servant of all. Then He took a child in His arms and said, "Whosoever shall receive one of such children in my name, receiveth me" (Mark 9:37).

The struggle for supremacy broke out again when the mother of James and John asked for the right-hand and left-hand places in the Kingdom for her sons. On the eve of the betrayal, the same strife flared which hindered every one of them from volunteering to wash the feet of the rest.

This ambition for the foremost place led Peter to insist, "Although all shall be offended, yet will not I....If I should die with thee, I will not deny thee" (Mark 14:29,31). He meant every word he spoke. His passionate devotion made him resolve that no hurt which he could prevent should touch his Lord. He knew in his heart that it would be easier and far better to die with Christ than to live without Him.

When the Lord gave instruction on the duty of forgiveness, Peter broke in with the inquiry, "Lord, how oft shall my brother sin against me, and I forgive him?" (Matthew 18:21). He suggested that seven times was the limit that he could not be expected to exceed. Our Lord swept away the suggestion as unthinkable. Calvary and Pentecost would open the gates of unlimited mercy. "Jesus saith unto him, I say not unto thee, Until seven times: but, Until seventy times seven" (Matthew 18:22).

In the parable of the unforgiving servant which followed, sin against another person was contrasted with the enormity of sin against God. Divine compassion releases and forgives debts of ten thousand talents. Jesus said nothing of the cost in ransom blood which He would soon be paying in flowing streams from His own heart.

Our Lord knew that an hour was near when Peter would find himself guilty of a ten thousand talent sin. At such a time he would cling to the hope suggested by this parable as a drowning man clings to the rope thrown out for his rescue.

Years later Peter wrote, "Love as brethren, be pitiful, be courteous: Not rendering evil for evil but contrariwise blessing....His own self bare our sins in his own body on the tree....Charity shall cover the multitude of sins" (1 Peter 3:8-9; 2:24; 4:8).

When the rich young man, unable to pay the price

of discipleship, had turned sorrowfully away, Peter broke in on the Savior's disappointment with the question, "Behold, we have forsaken all, and followed thee; what shall we have therefore?" (Matthew 19:27). Surely a handsome return awaited them for the sacrifices that discipleship had involved. But bargaining in this way was not permitted in the Kingdom of heaven. Therefore, Jesus used the parable of the laborers in the vineyard to teach that, in the service of God, a spirit of trust in His grace must overcome a spirit of bargaining.

The laborers had waited in the marketplace from early dawn, but no man had hired them. Not until almost sundown did they have their chance to work. But when, after one brief hour of service, they came to be paid, they received a whole day's pay. Their reward was not considered a debt but a gift of grace.

It was as if our Lord had said, "You did come early into the vineyard. You have borne the burden and heat of the day. But you have only done your duty, and your reward will be according to the riches of God's grace."

Jesus knew that approaching with the Passover was the treachery of Judas, the denial by Peter, and the desertion of all the disciples. With this knowledge was blended an over-brimming love. "Having loved his own which were in the world, he loved them unto the end" (John 13:1). Jesus was more concerned for His own, and especially for Peter, than for Himself. Therefore, He took several precautions that would strengthen Peter in the days to come.

Jesus knew the priceless worth of friendship. He made no secret of the tender intimacy which knit His soul with John. More than any other, John has interpreted to the world the secret workings of Jesus' heart.

Jesus could trust John entirely. The ultimate proof of His confidence was given when, from the cross, He committed His mother to the care of His beloved friend. He knew what John's friendship would mean to Peter in the hour of darkness, and therefore, He placed them together in His last sacred commission. "He sent Peter and John, saying, Go and prepare us the passover, that we may eat" (Luke 22:8). Thus He set His seal on their old-time friendship.

Together Peter and John had left their homes and nets to follow Jesus. They had probably been attracted to each other by an instinctive consciousness that each supplied personal qualities that the other lacked. With James, the brother of John, they had shared in the miraculous catch of fish and watched as the daughter of Jairus awoke from death beneath the touch of Jesus. They saw the wonder of the transfiguration and listened as Jesus unveiled the signs of the end of the age.

Our Lord had noticed and rejoiced in their comradeship. He knew how much it would mean for both them and for the gospel when His physical presence was withdrawn. He, therefore, made a special effort to cement and bless their friendship by this expression of confidence.

The result justified His fond anticipations. Peter

naturally turned to John when the storm of guilt and remorse was expending its full fury on his soul. It is not good that man should be alone, especially in hours when he remembers his sins and is distracted with inner warfare. The Lord anticipates such need. Before it arises, He provides a Jonathan for David, a John for Peter, a Timothy for Paul, and a faithful friend for the troubled Christian.

Chapter 7

FINAL EXHORTATION AND COMFORT

Jesus had greatly desired to eat the Passover supper with His disciples before He suffered. He entrusted the preparations to His two devoted friends, Peter and John. Deeply impressed with the seriousness of the responsibility, they secured the lamb, brought it to the priest for killing, purchased the bitter herbs, Passover cakes, and a skin of wine, and hastened back to prepare the meal.

The city was too preoccupied and crowded to notice the famous Teacher and His companions as they passed through the gate on their way to the appointed meeting place. The sky was already darkening, and stars were beginning to appear. Apparently, the embers of jealous rivalry were still smoldering also, and it burst into a flame as soon as the disciples arrived at the large upper room.

The walk had been hot and dusty. Pitcher, basin, and towel were provided, but no apostle volunteered to perform the custom of foot washing for the rest. To undertake the menial duty would, in their judgment, be equivalent to signing a deed of abdication from the throne of power which each was claiming. Besides, the seating arrangements at the table had to be considered. Even if the place on the Lord's right hand was conceded to John, who should be on His left?

Tension filled the room, and the peaceful enjoyment of the feast, on which Jesus had placed such importance, was seriously threatened. To end any further discussion, the Lord arose from the supper table and laid aside His outer garments. He girded Himself with the towel, as any household servant might have done, poured water into the basin, and began to wash His disciples' feet.

A sudden silence must have fallen over the group as He passed from one to another in this lowly ministry. Then He came to Peter who had been watching the process with shame and indignation. "Lord, dost thou wash my feet?...Thou shalt never wash my feet" (John 13:6,8). How little he realized that a still more drastic cleansing must soon be administered by those gentle hands, or he could have no part with Jesus in the mission of redemption.

"If I wash thee not, thou hast no part with me" (John 13:8). Evidently Peter understood his Master's meaning. The outward was symbolic of the inward, and the physical was symbolic of the spiritual.

He replied, "Lord, not my feet only, but also my hands and my head" (John 13:9).

"No," said Jesus. "That is not necessary. It is sufficient for the soiled members to be cleansed, and the body is completely clean. When My disciples fall into sin, there is no need for them to begin their spiritual life afresh. Whenever confession is made and cleansing sought, I will be faithful and just to forgive the sin and cleanse from all unrighteousness."

Therefore, a double significance was evident in our Lord's lowly act of feet washing. He taught the royalty of service and also that sin does not sever the regenerate soul from God. The disciple is still a disciple; the child is still a child. There must be confession, and there will be instant restoration. "Restore such an one in the spirit of meekness; considering thyself, lest thou also be tempted" (Galatians 6:1).

What a wealth of comfort has been ministered by this lowly act of the Savior to those whose feet have become soiled by the dust of earth's highways! Washing the feet of these simple men did not seem incongruous with the throne to which He went. Now that Jesus is on the throne, He will turn aside from the adoration of eternity and listen for every sigh of a contrite spirit.

A blast from the silver trumpets of the temple gave the signal for the Passover supper to begin in all parts of the city. On the table were the bread, wine, herbs, and roasted lamb. For hundreds of years the same customs had been followed, the same psalms sung, the same blessings and thanksgivings pronounced. The apostles were conscious that a heavy cloud was upon the Master's soul. He said, "Verily, verily, I say unto you, that one of you shall betray me" (John 13:21).

Each disciple, except Judas, suspected himself more than any of his fellows and said fearfully, "Master, is it I?" Peter, impatient of the uncertainty and perhaps anxious to be sure that it was not him, made a secret sign to John to ask to whom the Lord had referred. In a whisper, John asked who the traitor would be.

Jesus replied quietly so that probably only Peter, John, and Judas heard. "He it is, to whom I shall give a sop, when I have dipped it" (John 13:26). Then, placing some bitter herbs between slices of bread, He dipped the morsel into a special bowl of mixed fruits and passed it to Judas.

The traitor realized that the Master knew his intentions, but he arrogantly said, "Master, is it I?"

Under His breath our Lord replied, "It is as thou hast said." Then louder, so that everyone around the table heard, He said, "That thou doest, do quickly" (John 13:27).

The traitor could no longer bear the light of Christ's holy presence. Perhaps remorse had already begun to gnaw at his stomach. Hastily wrapping his cloak around him, he went out into the night. The revealing words had been spoken so gently that even Peter and John did not suspect that the thirty pieces of silver—the price of blood—were already in Judas' purse. He had played his part so well that the rest supposed that the Lord had commissioned him to buy some additional food for the feast, or that he had gone out to make an offering to the poor.

In later years, Peter compared the devil to a lion

roaring around the sheepfold and seeking an unguarded opening or a stray sheep. As he wrote the words, he must have had in mind the Master's warning, "Simon, Simon, behold, Satan hath desired to have you, that he may sift you as wheat: But I have prayed for thee, that thy faith fail not" (Luke 22:31-32).

The Savior's words are full of comfort. Satan has to obtain permission before he sifts, and there is a limit beyond which he may not go. "God is faithful," says the apostle, "who will not suffer you to be tempted above that ye are able" (1 Corinthians 10:13). Hosts of evil spirits hover around our path, awaiting the favorable moment for enticing us to sin. They hate us because evil hates goodness and because in our failure they can cause grief to the Captain of our salvation. But greater is He that is for us than all that are against us.

Temptation reveals our weakness and drives us in repentance and faith to Christ. There is no sin in being attacked by the evil one. We cannot help being tempted. But we can resist steadfast in the faith and appropriate grace in Christ so that we become more than conquerors. Throughout the conflict, we are conscious of our Savior's intercession. "Thanks be to God which giveth us the victory through our Lord Jesus Christ" (1 Corinthians 15:57).

Peter asked Jesus, "Lord, why cannot I follow thee now? I will lay down my life for thy sake. Jesus answered him, Wilt thou lay down thy life for my sake? Verily, verily, I say unto thee, The cock shall not crow, till thou hast denied me thrice'' (John 13:37-38). Then He said, ''Let not your heart be troubled....In my Father's house are many mansions....I go to prepare a place for you'' (John 14:1-2).

The ''many mansions'' suggest not only spaciousness but room for each character and individual to develop. The saints will have room to be themselves, and each will have enough love, joy, space, together with his own share of the fullness and service of Christ. Peter will still be Peter. Each star will differ from all the rest. There will be many mansions and no need to contend for room.

The significance of our Lord's promise is clearly defined when we remember that He predicted, only a few minutes earlier, that one would deny and all would forsake Him. ''I go to prepare a place for you,'' He said. ''For you, my beloved John; for you, Peter, when the memory of your denial will pass away; for you, Thomas, although you are given to doubt and pessimism; for you, Philip, longing to be shown the Father. Not one of you will be overlooked, and not one will miss his share. Let not your heart be troubled, neither let it be afraid.''

We may take courage if we are trusting Jesus for His justifying grace. In spite of our sins and failures, our sorrows and temptations, He will bring us through. ''Whom he called, them he also justified: and whom he justified, them he also glorified. What shall we then say to these things? If God be for us, who can be against us?'' (Romans 8:30-31).

Chapter 8

RENEWED BY HIS LOVE

In the Song of Solomon three traits are assigned to a perfect love. Each of these was notably present in our Lord's treatment of His apostle and friend who had been warned three times, had denied Him three times, and on three different occasions was restored.

"Love is strong as death" (Song of Solomon 8:6). At His own request, Jesus had been made sin for man, that God might be the justifier of them who believed. He laid down His life, and, by death, destroyed him that had the power of death. He ascended from His grave, robbing death of its sting and the grave of its victory.

Jesus' love is strong. In others it may be merely emotional affection, expressing itself in smiles, tears, tenderness, and largely composed of sentiment; but Christ's love is strong as well as tender. He is immortal love, but He is the strong Son of God.

Jesus loves us as He loved Peter, Mary, and John. He understands our failures and calls us by name, back from our wanderings. "Many waters cannot quench love" (Song of Solomon 8:7). Christ's love burns brightly although it has been beset by floods of ingratitude, indifference, waywardness, denial, and sin.

Descending from the upper room to the street by the outer staircase, Jesus led His disciples across the Kedron and up the slopes of Olivet. They had come here with Him often and were somewhat startled when He told eight of them to wait at the entrance while the other three were invited to advance farther along the grassy path. Jesus urged them to unite in watching and praying while He went a stone's throw from them. Not even the beloved John could be there when He took the cup from His Father's hand.

"Watch with me," He said as He left them. The request was prompted by His humanity, for who does not know the priceless value of sympathy in the painful times of life? Jesus knew also that it was the hour of darkness. Already Judas was calling his accomplices together.

But as Jesus returned three times to His disciples, He found them asleep. Finally, an angel had to furnish the comfort which man failed to give Him. Could Peter ever forget the Master's remonstrance which was addressed especially to him, "What, could ye not watch with me one hour?" (Matthew 26:40).

When Judas approached with the chief priests, scribes, and Pharisees, the apostles misread the situation. The approach of the armed company did not surprise them because Jesus had taught them to expect opposition. They had even brought along two swords. But they did not expect that a battle would be necessary. At the supreme moment, God would surely intervene, angels would appear on the scene, and their foes would be scattered.

Although Peter later quailed before the servant girl, he was not a coward. He would have fought like a lion if the Lord had permitted it. The others, when they realized the situation, asked the Master to give the signal to begin the fight. Not waiting for the Master's instructions, Peter was already in the midst of the throng, his sword flashing in the moonlight. He struck a mighty blow on the helmet of Malchus and severed his right ear.

Peter's action was well meant, but it could not be permitted. The dignity of the Savior's voluntary surrender would be impaired, and His deliberate acceptance of the cross would be clouded. The Pharisees would be only too glad to interpret their resistance as the beginning of a revolt against the Roman occupation.

Jesus had repeatedly insisted that no one took His life from Him but that He laid it down Himself. The voluntary element in His suffering would be lost if He were led off after a fierce struggle. He held back His followers, healed the wounded man, and then allowed them to lead Him away as a lamb to the slaughter.

The scribes and Pharisees, with their captive in

their midst, turned back to the city. John first recovered from his panic-stricken flight and followed closely in the rear, while Peter followed at a distance. On the opening of the great gates of Annas' palace, where the first informal trial for extracting further evidence was held, John entered with the crowd. Although he did not see Peter, he felt sure that his friend was waiting outside. He went back and spoke to the maid who recognized him as an acquaintance of the High Priest. She quickly admitted Peter, scanning his features as he passed under the oil-lamp that lighted the porch.

This porch led to an open quadrangle. The night was cold, and the servants kindled a fire which shed its flickering rays on the faces of the group that had shared in the night's adventure. Roman soldiers, Hebrew police, the servants of the High Priest, and the spies and informers who were waiting to give evidence stood and warmed themselves. John had gone into the council chamber, the windows of which looked out on the quadrangle; but Peter joined the group around the fire. He had lost heart and hope. His Master's rejection of his help in the garden had disconcerted him.

The gate-keeper who had admitted him left her post, came to the fire, recognized Peter, and accused him before the entire circle. "This man also was with the Galilean." He was taken by surprise but parried the attack by professing that he did not understand what she meant—"I know not, neither understand I what thou sayest" (Mark 14:68).

159

He quickly withdrew to the porch. As he reached it, a cock crowed in the grey dawn. There he was recognized by another maid who had probably heard the words of her fellow-servant at the fire. She remarked to a group of bystanders, "This fellow was also with Jesus of Nazareth. And again he denied with an oath, I do not know the man" (Matthew 26:71-72).

An hour later, he was back again at the fire, perhaps with the intention of vindicating his Master, even though he did not identify himself with His cause. But when he opened his mouth, his Galilean accent disproved his repeated and emphatic disavowals of any attachment to Jesus. The situation was extremely threatening, and Peter began to curse and swear, saying, "I know not this man of whom ye speak" (Mark 14:71).

A second time, while he was speaking, a cock crowed. Peter remembered the words that Jesus had spoken. Jesus also heard his loud cursing from where He was standing in the council chambers. Forgetting His own grief, He turned and looked at Peter, not with anger or reproach, but remembering and reminding.

And yet, after Jesus had risen from the dead, the angel said to the women at the tomb, "Tell his disciples and Peter" (Mark 16:7). Nothing can stop His love! We, too, may fail Him and deny Him. But when our hearts turn back in an agony of grief and remorse, He will renew us again.

Only those who have suffered keen remorse will

comprehend the anguish Peter felt as he fled the hateful scene of his denial. That last look of tender, pitying love haunted him! Could he ever forgive himself? Why had he not kept away from the fire or at least left the scene when he was first recognized?

He returned to John's house. The morning hours passed slowly. He could hear that the city was in an uproar, but only snatches of information floated through the open window. "Crucify" was shouted from ten thousand throats, and then the name "Barabbas."

About noon, heavy footsteps sounded in the doorway, and John came in supporting, almost carrying, Mary, Jesus' mother. When he looked at her agonized face, he learned that the worst had happened. Neither Mary nor John knew at that time that he was carrying a heavier load than they.

In the following hours, Peter confided the tragic story of his denial of the Lord. Blessed are they who under such circumstances have a friend like John. Blessed also are they who, remembering their own failures and weakness, can lovingly bind up broken hearts. "If a man be overtaken in fault, ye which are spiritual, restore such an one in the spirit of meekness; considering thyself, lest thou also be tempted. Bear ye one another's burdens, and so fulfill the law of Christ" (Galatians 1:6).

Early on Easter morning Mary of Magdala, breathless with haste, broke in on the sleepless anguish of John's home with the news that the body had been taken from its tomb. "They have taken away the Lord out of the sepulchre, and we know not where they have laid him" (John 20:2).

Instantly Peter was on his feet and rushed out, followed by John. They ran for the garden. Reaching the tomb first, John contented himself with looking in. But Peter, true to his impulsive nature, went straight into the chamber. The careful placement of the wrappings made it obvious that the body had not been stolen. John almost guessed the truth, and Peter became thoughtful. But they needed further confirmation, for they did not know the Scripture that He must rise again from the dead. They returned to their own home.

Later that day, the women broke in on them like a ray of the sunshine through a cloudy sky. They had seen an angel who gave them a message from the Lord! The angel told them to inform His brethren *and Peter* that Jesus was risen and would meet them in Galilee. (See Mark 16:7.)

The women had no idea of the impact of those words. They looked on Peter as foremost among the disciples, and it seemed quite fitting that he should be specifically mentioned in the angel's message. But to Peter, the mention of his name was as life from the dead. He insisted that the women repeat the whole wonderful story with every detail. When they left him to tell the others, he quietly adored the love that would not let him go—the love that never failed until it had found and brought back the sheep that had gone astray.

Chapter 9

WITNESSES OF THE RESURRECTION

In obedience to their Master's words, the apostles returned to Galilee. The time of their next meeting with the Lord was unknown. Therefore, when Peter proposed to resume their former trade, saying, "I'm going fishing," they immediately replied, "We will come with you." (See John 21:3.)

They got their boats and nets and set off for the familiar fishing grounds. The silence of the night was broken only by the casting of the nets and the occasional stroke of the oar. But when the grey morning began to dawn, they had caught nothing.

The disappointment was hard to bear. But those who have experienced God's dealings know that one door is shut that another may be opened. Our plans may fail because God has provided something wiser and better. Had the fishermen been successful that night, it would have been difficult to win them back to a life of dependence on their Master's personal care.

The disciples failed to recognize Jesus standing on

the sandy shore, wrapped in the golden shimmer of the morning mist. They thought that He was an early fish dealer.

But when He called out to them to cast their net on the right side, and it immediately filled with fish, John knew it was the Lord. He whispered his glad discovery to Peter. True to his impulsive nature, Peter threw himself into the sea and swam to shore. The other disciples followed in the boat, dragging the net which was heavy with their catch.

They gathered around the Lord as He prepared a meal of fish and bread, waiting expectantly for Him to tell them what to do next. But Jesus turned to Peter, seeking to obtain a decisive confession of his devotion to the Master so that all the disciples could hear.

Had it not been for the denial, none of the apostles would have questioned Peter's love for the Master. But now a shadow of doubt settled over their hearts. Our Lord realized this and knew that before He trusted Peter to tend His sheep, He must secure a decisive expression of the love which He knew was in His apostle's heart.

Only those who love can satisfy the requirements of Christ's service. Therefore, the Master asked persistently, "Do you love Me?" To the repeated question, Peter returned the same reply, "You know that I love You." He added the third time, "You know it not only with the perfect knowledge of God but with the intuitive sympathy of man." (See John 21:15-17.)

Peter staked everything on his Lord's intimate knowledge of the thoughts and intents of his heart. Clearly the Master had no doubt about His servant's loyalty, or He would never have entrusted him with the important responsibilities of the early Church.

Love alone, however, would not carry Peter through the trying times that lay ahead. He needed the same unwavering courage that had permeated Jesus' character. From the beginning, our Lord saw the cross standing on the horizon before Him. While facing a terrible death, Jesus never flinched or lost His composure. He remained obedient to His Father's will and plan.

This was to be Peter's experience also. "Thou shalt stretch forth thy hands, and another shall gird thee, and carry thee whither thou wouldst not. This spake he, signifying by what death he should glorify God" (John 21:19).

In his proud self-confidence, Peter once said, "Lord, I am ready to go with thee, both into prison, and to death" (Luke 22:33).

The Savior replied, "Thou canst not follow me now; but thou shalt follow me afterwards" (John 13:36).

In his second epistle, Peter refers to these words of Jesus: "Knowing that shortly I must put off this my tabernacle, even as our Lord Jesus Christ hath shewed me" (2 Peter 1:14). Clearly for him also the cross was the ultimate goal; but he never swerved from the chosen path of service. The courage that could stand that strain was of rare and splendid quality, and it proved his fitness for leadership.

With his fellow disciples, Peter returned from the scene of the ascension to the city with great joy. He realized that the blessed fellowship of the last six weeks was now ended and that his Master had gone to the Father. Yet, the evidence of His great power and glory, the assurance that they were to be filled with the power of the Comforter within the next few days, and the belief that Jesus would come again were sufficient to fill them with joy and triumph.

They returned to the upper room which was filled to capacity when the entire group of apostles, disciples, and holy women were assembled. Peter acted as moderator for the meeting although the Lord Himself was recognized by them all as still present. Peter defined the special work which lay before them, as it had been outlined by the Lord during the previous days. They were to be witnesses to the fact of the resurrection of their Lord. He said, "Beginning from the baptism of John, unto that same day that he was taken up from us, must one be ordained to be a witness with us of his resurrection" (Acts 1:22).

The word translated witness is *martyr*. So many of the early witnesses sealed their testimony with their blood, that the word became synonymous with the yielding up of life amid the horrors of fire, sword, the prison-cell, and the arena. We cannot utter the word lightly.

The resurrection of Jesus is not primarily to be

argued as a doctrine—it is a fact. It was the fitting consummation of the work of Jesus and is consistent with the anticipation of the prophets. But, primarily, it is a historical fact, communicated and vouched for by a number of witnesses.

Before our Lord began His ministry, He was anointed with the Holy Spirit and returned from the wilderness in the power of the Spirit to Galilee. That was our Savior's Pentecost. How much more must His followers receive the blessing of Pentecost that they might truly be known as Christians—anointed ones!

Jesus had promised His disciples: "And I will pray the Father, and he shall give you another Comforter, that he may abide with you for ever; Even the Spirit of truth" (John 14:16-17). Day after day they waited, worshipping God with great joy and wondering when and how the promised gift of power would be bestowed. Each day they expected, but for ten days patience was given the opportunity of perfecting her work.

The first day of the week marked the beginning of a celebration for the Jews. The priests in the special temple service would present the first fruits of the new harvest to God. The city was crowded with people from all over the world. It was a time of feasting and jubilant processions.

Early that morning, the embryo Church was assembled. Suddenly, a sound from heaven, like mighty rushing wind, startled the entire city. A globe of fire appeared, and it broke into tongues of flame that rested on each of them. Perhaps some of them remembered the words of John the Baptist: "He that cometh after me is mightier than I, whose shoes I am not worthy to bear: he shall baptize you with the Holy Ghost and with fire" (Matthew 3:11). The whole company was filled and began to speak with other tongues.

Meanwhile, summoned by the extraordinary sound, a crowd of Jews and proselytes gathered. As this torrent of excited and questioning multitudes poured into the area, they were met by the newly-anointed disciples. With the confidence their new experience had given, they proclaimed the risen glory of Jesus, speaking in the foreigners' native languages.

Then Peter stood up and addressed the multitude. His sermon was little more than the citation of long passages of Scripture, accompanied by brief comments. But the effect was extraordinary. As this Galilean fisherman began to speak, the mob suddenly became a congregation. Waves of tumultuous emotion filled the air, and the crowd became as one body, swayed and inspired by a common impulse. From the entire congregation the entreaty arose, "Men and brethren, what shall we do?" (Acts 2:37).

Why should we go on year after year without claiming our share in this Pentecostal power? Why do we fail to make use of that vast spiritual dynamo of Pentecost? We are not limited by God, but by ourselves. We do not have because we do not ask.

Every believer may share in the Pentecostal gift.

The Spirit may be in us, regenerating and renewing from within. But He should be on us also, as He descended and remained on Jesus in His Baptism, if we are to fulfill our ministry to mankind. No studying, no polished speech, no amount of evangelical teaching except by the Holy Spirit can be used for preaching the gospel. We must learn to say with Jesus, "The Spirit of the Lord is upon me, because he hath anointed me" (Luke 4:18).

Humbly open your heart to the blessed Spirit who changes the timid into courageous witnesses and makes the weak become as mighty as the angel of the Lord.

Chapter 10

THE POWER OF THE NAME

No great work of salvation or renewal is possible apart from the clear proclamation, first of the name of Jesus and second, of faith in His name. The name *and* faith in the name are both essential. Beneath the teaching of the Holy Spirit, Peter had learned this lesson well. In his second great sermon, he announced the eternal truth that the nature of the risen Lord, appropriated by a living faith, will bring healing.

The temple in Jerusalem was enclosed in three marble courts, rising in successive levels from street level. At the top of the second stairway, which only Jewish men could ascend, stood the Beautiful Gate which opened to the temple. The gate was made of brass and richly overlaid with plates of gold and silver. It took the strength of twenty men to open and close its massive leaves. But beauty alone can never inspire life or health—this was evident by the presence of an unfortunate beggar, now more than forty years of age, who from his birth had never walked.

He spent his days in the same spot, begging a pittance from the crowds that passed him through the gate to the temple.

As Peter climbed the temple steps on his way to the afternoon service, he saw the glory of the magnificent structure in all its splendor. He also saw the familiar sight of this miserable lame man. But he caught a glimpse of something else which was hidden from unanointed eyes. Being in the Spirit, the secrets of the spiritual world were open to him, and he beheld that crippled life as God meant it to be—whole, healthy, vigorous, and full of the music of perfected human vitality.

But faith in the name of Jesus must be called into operation before the lame man could obtain that perfect health which was in the Prince of Life. Led by a divine prompting, Peter suddenly realized that the man had faith for salvation. By his words and actions, Peter called it into expression. "Silver and gold have I none; but such as I have give I unto thee: In the name of Jesus Christ of Nazareth rise up and walk" (Acts 3:6). He took him by the right hand and raised him up.

Immediately the man's faith sprang into vigorous exercise. His feet and ankle-bones *received* strength. He entered the temple with Peter and John, "walking, and leaping, and praising God. And all the people saw him walking and praising God: And they knew that it was he which sat for alms at the Beautiful gate of the temple: and they were filled with wonder and amazement at that which had happened unto him'' (Acts 3:8-10). A crowd of people followed, and in reply to the buzz of questioning and awestruck wonder, Peter delivered his second sermon.

He turned the thoughts of his audience from John and himself to their Lord. It was not by their power or holiness that the man was healed but by the power of Him whom they had denied in the presence of Pilate. The evidence of Christ's resurrection was not only based on His apostles' words, but on the fact that the miracle done for the lame man was evident to them all. From that point he earnestly pled that they would repent so that their sins might be blotted out.

Peter was still addressing the hushed crowd when a group of officials moved toward the congregation, threaded its way through the mob, and arrested the three men. The Sadducees, who did not believe in the world of the Spirit or in the doctrine of a life after death, were probably responsible for this act. They had special reasons for resenting the teaching which the apostles had been spreading throughout Jerusalem. "Being grieved that they taught the people, and preached through Jesus the resurrection of the dead'' (Acts 4:2). If the resurrection proclaimed by Peter and his friends had actually happened, Sadduceeism would have ended.

Before Jerusalem was aware of what was happening, the apostles and the healed man were locked in prison, and messengers were hastening throughout the city to summon the members of the Sanhedrin to meet early the following morning.

That night must have been one of intense emotion for the imprisoned trio. This was the treatment their Master had taught them to expect. Peter remembered that he had vowed to follow Jesus to prison, and here was the chance of fulfilling his promise. They had no anxiety about the impending trial, as the words spoken three years earlier came back to them: "But when they deliver you up, take no thought how or what ye shall speak: for it shall be given you in that same hour what ye shall speak. For it is not ye that speak, but the Spirit of your Father that speaketh in you" (Matthew 10:19-20).

The Sanhedrin with its seventy elders was the most venerable and authoritative court in the world. The High Priest presided, and around him sat the heads of the twenty-four priestly classes, the doctors of the law, and the fathers of ancient Jewish families. It was the same body that had handed Jesus of Nazareth to the Roman executioners. Now, they were preparing to stamp out the Galilean heresy forever.

It was vain for them to question the miracle— the healed man was standing there before them. They avoided the general question of the resurrection because on this matter there was a division between the Pharisees and the Sadducees. But the point at issue was the *source* of his healing.

They asked, "By what power or by what name, have ye done this?" (Acts 4:7). If Peter and his associates had ascribed the miracle to the mighty power of Jehovah, nothing more could have been said. But if it were attributed to some other name, the apostles would bring themselves under the ancient penalty of death as sorcerers. If they ascribed it to Jesus, they would risk the death that had already been inflicted on Him.

Peter was oblivious to all questions of policy, and under the anointing of the divine Spirit, he said, "Rulers of the people, and elders of Israel, If we this day be examined of the good deed done to the impotent man, by what means he is made whole; Be it known unto you all...that by the name of Jesus Christ of Nazareth, whom ye crucified, whom God raised from the dead, even by him doth this man stand here before you whole. This is the stone which was set at nought of you builders, which is become the head of the corner. Neither is there salvation in any other" (Acts 4:8-12).

The reference to this rejected headstone recalled an ancient tradition. When Solomon built his famous temple, all the masonry was performed at a distance. Neither hammers, axe, nor any tool was heard during its construction. One day a huge stone was delivered from the quarry. Because of its unusual shape, it was obvious that considerable care had been expended on it. But no one could suggest the precise place in the structure it was intended to fill.

It was put aside as a misfit and lay on the site unrecognized and useless.

But when the building began to emerge above ground, a cornerstone was needed of a particular shape. Someone remembered the rejected stone, which, when it was placed in the gap, fit perfectly. The memory of this incident was preserved in the words: "The stone which the builders refused is become the headstone of the corner" (Psalm 118:22). Paul referred to it in addressing the Ephesian church: "Built upon the foundation of the apostles and prophets, Jesus Christ himself being the chief cornerstone" (Ephesians 2:20).

If a nation refuses to build according to the great truths that Jesus taught, it must pass on as all the great empires of the world—Babylonian, Persian, Grecian, and Roman—have passed on and become as dust. The only hope of salvation for any nation is to be built on the foundation of the gospel of the Son of Man.

Likewise, the church which substitutes doctrinal formularies, pomp and splendor of ritual, learning, or wealth for a vital contact with Jesus Christ may enjoy temporary success; but it will not endure. The only salvation for any church is in union with Jesus Christ.

Too many people diligently build their lives and businesses while they neglect Christ. They have no need or use for Him. But they cannot continue. For a while they flourish and grow, but eventually they are gone and forgotten. The life which is based on Christ and His teaching and example will shine as the stars forever. But those who reject or neglect Him are like the chaff which the wind drives away.

Jesus is the Rock. He is the living stone. He gives eternal life and unchanging stability! Elsewhere you may get philosophy, moral integrity, or virtue, but there is no other name given under heaven and among men whereby we must be saved.

As the Sanhedrin listened to Peter's words and watched the two apostles closely, they were reminded of Jesus. In their private conference, they agreed that they dare not permit these men to continue to preach and teach. They could not deny the miracle or disprove the resurrection, but they had to take some action. When the apostles were called, they were strictly ordered not to speak in the name of Jesus. The judges would have been glad to punish them, but this would enrage the people. So they threatened them and let them go.

But Peter and John could do nothing else but bear witness to the things that they had heard and seen. This is what Paul meant in 2 Corinthians 5:14 when he said, in answer to the arguments of his friends, "The love of Christ constraineth us." Oh, that we would be on fire for the Lord as these early Christians!

Peter and John returned to their brethren who had doubtless spent the hours in prayer. They did not ask that God would eliminate the persecutor or save their lives. The only request was that they might have power to give an unfaltering testimony and that wonders and signs would be accomplished in the name of Jesus. "And when they had prayed, the place was shaken where they were assembled together; and they were all filled with the Holy Ghost, and they spake the word of God with boldness" (Acts 4:31).

Chapter 11

A LARGER FIELD OF HARVEST

In its earliest stages, the public sentiment of Jerusalem was strongly in favor of the Church. This was largely because of the miraculous works of healing that gathered crowds around the apostles, just as they had been drawn to the Lord Jesus. "They brought forth the sick into the streets, and laid them on beds and couches, that at the least the shadow of Peter passing by might overshadow some of them" (Acts 5:15). News spread throughout the land of the wondrous cures accomplished in the name of Jesus.

For a time the rulers stood rigidly aloof. But finally the smoldering embers of their jealousy burst into fire, and the whole apostolic band was arrested and thrust into the public prison. The following morning the Sanhedrin, reinforced by the senate of Israel, met to judge the matter. But the prison was empty, and news came that their prisoners were standing in the temple and teaching the people.

Despite the miraculous character of their liberation, the trial proceeded, and Peter had another opportunity to proclaim the resurrection of his Lord before the ruling classes. In his testimony, Peter placed a new emphasis on the confirming witness of the Holy Spirit. "We are his witnesses of these things; and so is also the Holy Ghost, whom God hath given to them that obey him" (Acts 5:32).

Although many members of the council wanted to kill the apostles, they were released after a severe beating and a warning to speak no more in the name of Jesus. "And they departed from the presence of the council, rejoicing that they were counted worthy to suffer shame for his name. And daily in the temple, and in every house, they ceased not to teach and preach Jesus Christ" (Acts 6:41-42).

From the beginning, the divine objective was to include Jews and Gentiles in one Church. Many of the apostles, however, supposed that Gentiles could only enter the Christian Church by first becoming Jews. When our Lord commissioned His apostles to go into all the world and make disciples from all the nations, they probably supposed that the rite of circumcision would precede baptism. Gradually, they began to understand that in Christ Jesus there is neither Jew nor Greek, circumcision nor uncircumcision, male nor female, but all are one in Him. (See Galatians 3:28 and Colossians 3:11.)

It was fitting that Peter, to whom the keys of the Kingdom were committed and who had opened the door of Pentecostal blessings to Jews, should fulfill the same ministry to the Gentiles also. For eight years with his fellow apostles, Peter had confined himself to the work of the Jerusalem church. He was now to learn that her children would be gathered from a great multitude of every nation, people, and tongue.

Peter was a strict Jew. He was inclined to view with suspicion even the Hellenist, or Greek-speaking, Jews who were scattered throughout the Roman Empire. He had never entered a Gentile home, never sat at a Gentile table, and never transgressed the Levitical dietary laws. The Lord patiently dealt with Peter, one step at a time, until he was at last ready to preach the gospel to the Gentiles.

A large contingent of Hellenist Jews were present on the day of Pentecost and had accepted Jesus as their Messiah. Many of them sold their possessions and joined the community of believers in Jerusalem. But suddenly the calm waters of peace and love became ruffled by dissatisfaction. Hellenist widows complained that partiality was shown in the daily distribution of food and that Hebrew women received more than they did.

The peril of a serious division in the church became imminent, and Peter and his brethren were compelled to take action. They concluded that their highest calling was to prayer and the ministry of the Word. The service of tables should be entrusted to seven men of good report who were full of the Holy Spirit and wisdom. "Look ye out among you seven men...whom we may appoint over this business. But we will give ourselves continually to prayer, and to the ministry of the word" (Acts 6:3-4).

All Hellenist Jews were chosen for the service with the exception of one, who was a Gentile proselyte. The unanimity of the church in this solemn act was obviously due to the presence and direction of the Spirit. Peter could say nothing to the contrary, although the choice of the Hellenists must have surprised him.

Stephen, the eloquent young Hellenist, probably made a great impression on Peter. He often listened to Stephen's burning words as he insisted that throughout their history the chosen people had resisted the divine Spirit when He summoned them to a new step of faith. As he listened, Peter may have recalled the Master's words, that it would be impossible to put the new wine in the old bottles. (See Mark 2:22.) He was being prepared for a deeper understanding of his Master's purpose.

The mission to Samaria followed. Beneath Philip's preaching, vast numbers of Samaritans had broken away from spiritualism and were baptized in the name of Jesus. Peter and John were sent to lead the new converts into the full enjoyment of the gifts of Pentecost. As Peter used the keys of teaching and prayer, the miracle of Pentecost was repeated. "They received the Holy Ghost." (Acts 8:17).

Samaritans were regarded by Jews as a mongrel race. Their name was used as an insult: "You lousy Samaritan!" A good deed like that attributed to the Good Samaritan was not generally expected from a race that was looked upon as accursed. But, to the obvious astonishment of the apostles, the Holy Spirit descended on these believing Samaritans with absolute impartiality. Peter was so impressed with what he saw that he could not oppose the divine purpose. Therefore, when he and John returned to Jerusalem, they preached in the villages of Samaria.

Meanwhile, a startling rumor had reached Jerusalem. Saul of Tarsus, the arch-persecutor of the Church, had been stopped by the direct intervention of the Lord and had become His humble follower. As the further details filtered in of this wonderful event, they learned that Saul had been forced to flee from Damascus and had gone to Arabia. Some time elapsed, and finally, to Peter's surprise, he presented himself at his humble dwelling in Jerusalem and remained as his guest for fifteen days.

These two men, so different in age, education, and experience, were closely united in Jesus Christ. Peter must have shared the details of his years with Jesus while Paul listened with rapt interest. But Paul's life was in danger in Jerusalem, and he could not remain there long. He told Peter that God called him to be "a chosen vessel unto me, to bear my name before the Gentiles, and kings, and the children of Israel" (Acts 9:15).

Peter immediately made arrangements for Paul to leave the danger zone for Caesarea and ultimately to Tarsus. When he was safely away, however, those parting words must have rung in Peter's heart: "Bear my name before the Gentiles." He could not challenge those words. They were spoken by the Master, and they further prepared him for the fresh demands which would soon be made on him.

After the departure of Paul, Peter visited some of the smaller congregations that were scattered throughout Judea. He came to Lydda where he lifted Eneas from eight years of paralysis. Then he was summoned by an urgent message to Joppa, six and a half miles away, where the beloved Dorcas had died. His prayer on her behalf prevailed with God. When he gave her his hand, she arose to continue her ministry to the saints and widows in the little town.

There, however, his work seemed finished. The Jerusalem church had been diminished by persecution, and there was little left for him to do. What was to be the next step in the fulfillment of his life-work? Was some new development of the divine pattern at hand which he must realize for himself and others?

One afternoon, when the blazing sunshine poured down on the white houses of Joppa, Peter went up to the housetop for prayer. There he caught the vision of a redeemed world, like a great white sheet. The variety of its contents—four-footed beasts, creeping things, birds clean and unclean—startled him. Even more astonishing was the declaration that God had cleansed them all. The old Levitical restrictions were removed, and any of them were fit for food. (See Acts 10:9-16.)

While he was puzzled about what the vision might mean, he heard a knock at the gate and the voices of men. The Spirit assured him that there was no need for fear or hesitation—it was time for him to lead the Church into the greatest revolution she had known since the ascension of her Lord.

What a lesson is here for our perplexed and anxious hearts! We find it difficult to wait for the Lord's timing. Although we pray, we do not trust. Let us rest in Him and believe that even now the messengers are hurrying to us with the direction or help we need.

"I will stand upon my watch, and set me upon the tower, and will watch to see what he will say unto me....For the vision is yet for an appointed time, but at the end it shall speak and not lie: though it tarry, wait for it; because it will surely come, it will not tarry....The just shall live by his faith" (Habakkuk 2:1,3-4).

Before we step out on an unknown path, let us wait for our visions to be confirmed by the clear voice of the Spirit. "While Peter thought on the vision, the Spirit said unto him, Behold, three men seek thee" (Acts 10:19). When you are doubtful whether your vision is from God, wait for the further indication of His will through circumstance. Then wait for the still, small voice of the Holy Spirit saying, "Arise therefore, and get thee down, and go with them, doubting nothing: for I have sent them" (Acts 10:20).

All Peter's doubts vanished. His hesitation was ended. He invited the three men in, and on the following morning, he started with them on the journey to Caesarea. He brought along six believing Jews, realizing that he was taking a step which would be closely scrutinized by the apostles and leaders at Jerusalem.

When it was announced that they had arrived, Cornelius met them at the outer gate. With instinctive reverence and courtesy, he prostrated himself before the man who had been commissioned by a message from God. Peter instantly stooped to raise him saying, "Stand up; I myself also am a man" (Acts 10:26).

They walked together to a large room where the expectant gathering awaited them. Amid the awed hush in an atmosphere charged with spiritual emotion, and with the consciousness that he was following some divine purpose, Peter began to speak. He told the well-known story of Jesus who came in the appearance of man but was Lord of all. Peter gave his personal testimony to Jesus' resurrection from the grave. Finally, he proclaimed the forgiveness and remission of sin through faith in His name.

Not a word was uttered about circumcision. There was no suggestion that they must pass through the synagogue to the Church. The one condition of forgiveness was faith in Him whom God raised from the dead.

Peter had only begun to speak when the Holy Spirit swept over the audience, as the summer breeze breathes over the rustling corn. The Spirit of God was eager to get to work and moved Peter gently aside. On the day of Pentecost, the apostle had time to develop his argument and drive home his appeal; but in this case neither was required. The Holy Spirit fell on all them which heard the Word. The six brethren who had accompanied Peter were amazed as they heard them speaking with tongues and magnifying God.

Peter said afterward that it reminded him of Pentecost. "As I began to speak, the Holy Ghost fell on them, as on us at the beginning. Then remembered I the word of the Lord how that he said, John indeed baptized with water; but ye shall be baptized with the Holy Ghost. Forasmuch then as God gave them the like gift as he did unto us, who believed on the Lord Jesus Christ; what was I, that I could withstand God?" (Acts 11:15-17).

The news of what Peter had done soon reached Jerusalem. He lost no time in returning to give his personal impression and report. The brethren throughout Judea heard that the Gentiles also received the Word of God. We may infer that the news caused great excitement and probably misunderstanding. A strong conservative party insisted that the Gentile must become a Jew before receiving Christ.

The apostles met the charges by a careful narration of the facts. The outpouring of the Spirit was the divine vindication of Peter's action. The sealing of the Spirit had been given to Gentiles just as to Jews who believed. Faith alone had been the requirement.

Surely, then, neither circumcision nor uncircumcision mattered. Nothing more could be said. "When they heard these things, they held their peace, and glorified God, saying, Then hath God also to the Gentiles granted repentance unto life" (Acts 11:18).

Chapter 12

FULFILLING A PROMISE

Again it was the Passover. Fourteen years had passed since Peter was sent with John to prepare the Passover feast for his Lord. That evening he had vowed to go with Jesus even to prison. The time had come for him to fulfill his vow.

"Now about that time Herod the king stretched forth his hands to vex certain of the church" (Acts 12:1). James, one of the Master's innermost circle, was the first to be executed. When Herod saw that it pleased the Jews, he was encouraged to strike again, but harder.

Peter was the strongest element in the Christian community. Herod had him arrested, and sixteen soldiers were commissioned to watch him. Two were in the cell with Peter, his hands fastened to one on either side. A third stood outside the bolted door, and the rest were posted along the corridor which led to the great iron gate.

The situation appeared desperate, so far as human judgment was concerned. If Herod succeeded in his plan against Peter, the Church could expect nothing less than a massacre. But with God all things are possible. "Peter therefore was kept in prison; but prayer was made without ceasing of the church unto God for him" (Acts 12:5).

Day after day passed, and the seven days of the feast expired. The next day, Herod would bring his prisoner forth to a mock trial and then a cruel death. As yet, there had been no answering voice from heaven. But the church never ceased its agonizing pleadings on Peter's behalf.

Meanwhile, the Lord was answering prayer by the great peace which He breathed into Peter's soul as he slept peacefully between two soldiers. Peter's letter written years later revealed the secret of his tranquility. He was experiencing the blessedness of those who are reproached for the name of Christ. He was permitted to be a partaker of Christ's sufferings. The Spirit of glory and of God was resting upon him. He was suffering according to the will of God and was happy to commit his soul to his faithful Creator. (See 1 Peter 4:12-14.)

Perhaps he pillowed his heart on the words which the Lord had addressed to him on the shores of the lake: "When thou shalt be old, thou shalt stretch forth thy hands, and another shall gird thee, and carry thee whither thou wouldest not" (John 21:18). Peter was not yet old. His work was not finished, and death by crucifixion was not in Herod's power. Therefore, he rested in the Lord and waited patiently for Him. His mind was kept in perfect peace.

God's angels are sent forth to minister to us who need their comfort and help. Except in extreme cases, they do not manifest themselves, but they are with us always. One angel had been at Peter's side for the whole seven days of his imprisonment, waiting for the precise moment fixed for action by the Lord. When it arrived, he cast off his enshrouding veil, and instantly a mild and gentle light fell on the sleeping group, awakening none of them. He had to strike Peter on his side and call him to arise. Peter awoke, hardly aware that the chains no longer held him. He must have been dazed and needed constant reminders of what he should do—tighten his belt, put on his sandals, and wrap his warm outer cloak around his shoulders. He passed through the door of the cell as though in a dream. He "wist not that it was true which was done by the angel; but thought he saw a vision" (Acts 12:9).

The gleaming light from his companion led him past the first and second sentries, but they gave no sign of awakening because a deep sleep from God had fallen upon them. When they reached the iron gates, this last barrier was swung open and closed again by strong and invisible hands. After they had passed through one street, the angel left him, "and when he had considered the thing, he came to the house of Mary...where many were gathered together praying" (Acts 12:12).

There had been no sleep in that home. Peter's coming martyrdom was on every heart. When Rhoda, the servant-girl, rushed into their midst with

190

the announcement that Peter was standing at the gate, they told her she was mad. But her confident affirmation and Peter's continued knocking at last prevailed. "When they had opened the door and saw him, they were astonished" (Acts 12:16).

Peter did not enter the house. As soon as the guards realized he was missing, a search would probably be instituted in the homes of his friends. There must be no presumption on his part. He must use his own wit to evade his foes. Therefore, with a few hurried explanations and directions, he departed while it was still dark and went to another place.

We all find ourselves in prison at times—the prison of circumstances from which we cannot extricate ourselves; of relationships that restrain our liberty; of consequences from past sins. Let us cry to the Lord in our trouble and ask Him to save us out of our distress. Let us confess our sins and turn to Him for help. He will hear our cry out of the lowest dungeon. He will send His angel to loosen our chains and open the prison doors. As Peter testified years later, "The Lord knoweth how to deliver the godly out of temptations, and to reserve the unjust unto the day of judgment to be punished" (2 Peter 2:9).

After his miraculous escape from prison, Peter concentrated his labors on the vast multitude of Israelites who were scattered through the Eastern portion of the Roman Empire. Representatives of the scattered Jews are mentioned in the second chapter of Acts as forming part of the vast crowd which gathered on the day of Pentecost. These same districts were probably included in the wide area which constituted Peter's territory. The last sixteen or seventeen years of his life were occupied by a wide system of evangelistic ministry. Accompanied by his devoted wife, he passed from place to place with such remarkable success that there was a widespread turning from idols to serve the living and true God.

Forty years after Peter's death, Pliny, governor of part of the region influenced by Peter, described in an official report the wonderful predominance of Christianity. The temples dedicated to Jupiter and Mars were deserted, and the usual sacrifices were unoffered; and, the entire population frequented the assemblies of "the pestilent Christian heresy." He acknowledged the purity and blamelessness of the Christian ideals and practice, their solemn oaths to abstain from sin, and their freedom from violence. This testimony is confirmed by others, and we obtain the vision of a widespread Christian community animated by passionate devotion to Christ and to the spread of His gospel.

A plentiful and rich harvest had resulted from the labors of Peter and his fellow-workers in these prolific fields. A vast area containing 500 cities and towns was repeatedly visited by the apostle. His epistles supply evidence that he remained long enough in each place to build healthy churches, appoint elders, and shepherd the sheep, according to the Lord's command. The tone of his letters is affectionate and intimate. He was sympathetic concerning the afflictions and sufferings they faced. A tender personal relationship knit them together.

Peter wrote his first letter from Babylon. (See 1 Peter 5:13.) When the increasing infirmities of age placed a necessary restraint on his labors, Peter may have made his home in that ancient and historic city, which was densely populated by Jews. His death apparently took place at Rome.

The Roman emperor Nero was determined to destroy the Church and promote ungodliness throughout the land. After reducing Rome to ashes by the inferno which his wanton cruelty had kindled, Nero cringed before the passionate resentment of his subjects. In his effort to divert it from himself, he blamed the hideous crime on the Christians. In his search for victims he scoured the empire, striking first and hardest the most illustrious and well-known Christian leaders. Among these Paul was certainly one, and Peter was almost certainly another.

What befell the apostles in Rome is not chronicled by Scripture. Dionysis, Bishop of Corinth in the second century, states that Peter and Paul suffered martyrdom at the same time. Jerome, in the fourth century, attests that Peter was crucified with his head turned earthward and his feet in the air, because he insisted that he was unworthy to be crucified as his Lord was. Certainly Jesus awaited His servant on the other side to give him a triumphant entrance into the Kingdom and glory of the Father.

Peter wrote to remind his brethren that they had been born again to a living hope by the resurrection of Jesus Christ from the dead. For them an inheritance had been purchased and was awaiting them which was incorruptible and undefiled. A salvation was ready to be revealed which would cause them to forget their heavy trials. Great grace was to be brought to them at the glorious unveiling of Jesus Christ. They had been partakers of Christ's sufferings, but His glory would certainly be revealed. Then they would rejoice and receive a crown of glory that could not fade away. They could confidently look forward to the new heavens and the new earth, "wherein dwelleth righteousness" (2 Peter 3:13). If Paul has been called the Apostle of Faith and John the Apostle of Love, surely Peter is rightly remembered as the Apostle of Hope.

Peter thought and spoke of death as the putting off of the tent or tabernacle, which symbolized the pilgrim character of his earthly life, that he might enter his permanent dwelling place, eternal in the heavens. For him death was not a condition but a passage.

He hoped that he and those whom he addressed might have a blessed entrance into Christ's eternal Kingdom and glory. But beyond this, he counted on the inheritance that was reserved in heaven for him and the glory to be revealed. All was summed up in the vision of that dear face, which he hoped to see as soon as he had crossed over. Jesus had been the day star of his heart, and Jesus would be the light of all his future. He would dwell forever in the City which needs neither sun nor moon, because the Lamb of God is the light.

PAUL: THE APOSTLE

Chapter 1

WHEN I WAS A CHILD

Near the eastern bay of the Mediterranean, in the midst of a rich and luxuriant plain, stood the city of Tarsus, a thriving center for trade and a focus of intellectual and religious activity. To the north rose the mighty Taurus mountains. Its peaks of eternal snow fed the river Cyndus which passed through the midst of the town and on to the sea. Large vessels brought the treasures of East and West to the wharves that lined either bank. Merchandise and commodities of every kind were brought here in exchange for goats' hair cloth.

While Jesus was still an infant in His mother's arms at Nazareth, a child was born in Tarsus. His life and his message was destined to give new meaning to men's religious convictions. At his circumcision he received a double name—Saul for his Hebrew family and Paul for the world of trade and municipal life.

Paul was reared amid busy streets and bazaars crowded with merchants, students, and sailors from all parts of the world. As the lad grew, he learned to understand every aspect of human life. He became familiar with the thoughts and habits of the marketplace, the camp, the arena, and the temple. Nothing that touched human life was foreign to him. He loved the stir of the city and later drew his metaphors from its keen interests.

Paul described himself as "a Hebrew of the Hebrews" (Philippians 3:5). There was no Gentile mixture in his blood. His father must have been a man of considerable position, or he would not have possessed the coveted birthright of Roman citizenship.

Paul's family probably spoke in the Hebrew tongue at home. This accounts for his intimate acquaintance with the Hebrew Scriptures he often quoted. Jesus spoke to him in Hebrew on the road to Damascus, and in Hebrew Paul later addressed some of the crowds who gathered around him.

Paul was proud to have the holy patriarchs and prophets as his ancestors. He held his head high as he remembered that he belonged to the chosen race. The adoption, the law, the service of God, and the promises all belonged to him.

His early education was deeply religious. He was "a Pharisee, the son of a Pharisee" (Acts 23:6). Today, the word Pharisee is a synonym for religious pride and hypocrisy; but then, the Pharisee represented the noblest traditions of the Hebrew people. Amid prevailing indifference, the Pharisees stood for a strict religious life. Against the skepticism of the Sadducees, who believed in neither spirit nor unseen world, the Pharisees held to the resurrection of the dead and the life of the world to come. The lax morals of the time infected Jerusalem almost as much as Rome, but the Pharisees remained strict and holy in their ideals.

Paul's early years were dominated by these strong religious convictions. As he heard of proselytes entering the covenant of his fathers, he congratulated himself that as a child he had been admitted into covenant relationship with God.

Paul was extremely zealous for his religious traditions. Concerning the righteousness which is of the law, so far as outward observances went, he was blameless. There was no precept in the moral or ceremonial law that he would consciously disregard. Although the rabbis had built upon the law of Moses an immense superstructure of commandments, he bravely set out to master them. He observed the Sabbath and festivals with the greatest care. "Brethren," he said on one occasion, "I have lived before God in all good conscience until this day" (Acts 23:1).

The ardent soul of the young Pharisee longed to stand in the front rank of the saints. Early in life he had made up his mind to win the prize of God's favor. He could imagine nothing more desirable than this. When, therefore, he learned that absolute obedience to the words of the rabbis was the only method of achieving his goal, he determined, with unremitting devotion, to succeed.

Paul must have been warm-hearted and fervid. His tears flowed at Miletus, and his heart nearly broke on his last journey to Jerusalem. Pathetic appeals to remain true to the faith filled his epistles, and he was blessed with many loyal friends. The contrast between the greetings to his many friends at the close of his letters and his silence about his parents, brothers, or sisters shows the bitterness of the final disowning that followed his conversion. There is more than appears on the surface in his remark, "For whom I have suffered the loss of all things" (Philippians 3:8).

The zeal that later led him to persecute the Church was already stirring in Paul's heart. He advanced in the Jewish faith beyond many his own age, being more zealous for the traditions of the fathers. He did not hold truth superficially but as a substance which had saturated the deepest emotions of his intense nature. He knew by personal experience what it was to have a zeal for God but not according to knowledge.

Paul's childhood must have passed in this way: at five he began to read the Scriptures; at six he was sent to the school of a neighboring rabbi; at ten he was instructed in the oral law; at thirteen he became a son of the law.

Between the ages of thirteen and sixteen, Paul went to Jerusalem to pursue his training for the office of rabbi. He had a married sister in Jerusalem with whom he lodged while attending the classes of the illustrious rabbi, Gamaliel.

Every Jewish boy was taught a trade, usually that of his father. Paul's family for generations had been engaged in weaving a dark, coarse cloth of goat's hair. From his childhood, he must have been familiar with the rattle of the looms as the long hair of the mountain goat was woven into a strong material, suitable for tents. This handicraft was perfect for the demands of a wandering life. Other trades required a settled workshop and expensive equipment, but this work could be performed anywhere and needed only a small amount of tools.

Fifty years later, confined in a Roman prison, Paul had time to review the things which he had previously counted as gain—his heritage, education, and careful attention to the law. As he counted up their treasures, he wrote across them—*loss.* "What things were gain to me, those I counted loss for Christ. Yea doubtless, and I count all things but loss for the excellency of the knowledge of Christ Jesus my Lord" (Philippians 3:7-8).

Paul had discovered that the sacrifices of Judaism could not remove sins. Outward rites, however carefully observed, did not cleanse the conscience. In Judaism there was no power for salvation, nothing to reinforce and renew the waning energies of the soul. Furthermore, he had found something better.

Paul had seen Jesus. Before the glory of that heavenly vision, all other objects of attraction had paled. In comparison with Christ's finished work, all his own efforts were futile. It was a relief to turn from his own righteousness of the law and to obtain true righteousness through faith in Christ.

Chapter 2

A SEED THAT PRODUCED MILLIONS

God introduces His greatest servants to the world in a variety of ways. They may rise gradually and majestically like the dawn to reach the brightness of mature power and usefulness. In other cases, they flash like the lightning on the dark abyss of night. God may charge a man with a message and launch him forth like Elijah, John the Baptist, and Stephen.

We know little of Stephen's background. He was a Hellenist Jew, and he probably had known the Son of Man. One day and one speech in his life was recorded. That day was his last, and that speech was his defense for his life.

Stephen's life and death must always attract our reverent interest; but how much more so as we trace his influence on the method, thought, and character of the great apostle whose life work it became to perpetuate the faith of the Church's first martyr.

Three streams of thought were meeting in tumultuous currents in Jerusalem at that time. First, there were the Pharisees, represented by Gamaliel, Saul of Tarsus, and other notable men. They were characterized by an intense religiousness that centered around their ancestry and their law. Intensely fanatical, they prided themselves on their privilege as the chosen people, but they resented the appeals of the greatest of their prophets. They depended on the effectiveness of their system of laws but were careless of personal character.

Next came the Hebrew Christian Church, led and represented by the apostles. To culture and eloquence, they had no claim. Of founding a new religious organization, they had no idea. They never expected to live to see Judaism superseded by the teaching they were giving or Christianity existing apart from the system in which they had been nurtured. Their Master had rigorously observed the Jewish rites and feasts, and they followed in His steps. If nothing had happened of the nature of Stephen's martyrdom, the Church would have become another Jewish sect, distinguished by the piety of its adherents and by their strange belief in the Messiahship of Jesus of Nazareth.

Lastly, there were the converts from among the Hellenist Jews. Of these, Stephen was the holy and eloquent member.

The Jews of Jerusalem and Judea shrank from the defiling touch of heathenism and built the wall of separation higher, growing continually more proud, bitter, and narrow. Meanwhile, the Jews that were scattered throughout the world became more liberal and cosmopolitan. They dropped their Hebrew mother tongue for Greek. They learned that although their fathers had received the holy oracles for mankind, God never left Himself without a witness. They welcomed all who called upon the name of their God.

After some years of absence, Paul returned to settle at Jerusalem. Perhaps its Jewish leaders, having been impressed by his remarkable talents and enthusiastic devotion to Judaism, had summoned him to lead the opposition to Christianity. It is almost certain that he was, at this time, nominated to a seat in the Sanhedrin; this enabled him to vote against the followers of Jesus. (See Acts 26:10.)

His first impression of the followers of "the Way," as the early disciples were called, was wholly unfavorable. It seemed to him sheer madness to suppose that the crucified Nazarene could be the long-awaited Messiah or that Jesus had risen from the dead. He, therefore, took the lead in disputing with Stephen, who had been raised to office in the growing Church. Discontent over the conservative and timid attitude of the apostles, Steven led an aggressive proclamation of the gospel.

Stephen's testimony was the first attempt to read the story of God's dealings with Israel in the light of Christ; the earliest commentary on the Old Testament by the New; the fragmentary draft of the epistle to the Hebrews; and the suggestion of a deeper way of studying the Mosaic laws.

Like most who speak God's truth for the first time, Stephen was greatly misunderstood. The Jewish leaders accused him of uttering blasphemous words against Moses, speaking against the temple and the law, and declaring that Jesus of Nazareth would destroy the temple and change the customs delivered by Moses. As we carefully follow his argument, we can see how these impressions had been caused.

Saul spoke on the glories of the temple as they stood on the site where Jehovah had been worshipped for centuries. But Stephen insisted that any holy soul could worship God in the temple of his own heart. Even Solomon acknowledged that God did not dwell in temples made with hands.

Saul insisted on the necessity of the rite of circumcision. But Stephen reminded him that God made promises to Abraham long before that rite was instituted.

Saul showed the unlikelihood of Jesus being God's Deliverer because He was unrecognized by the leaders of Israel. Stephen replied that there was nothing extraordinary in this, since Joseph had been sold by his brothers, and Moses was rejected on three distinct occasions. "Which of the prophets have not your fathers persecuted?" (Acts 7:52).

Saul said that all the prophets pointed to the glorious coming and reign of the Messiah. Stephen reviewed Moses, the Prophets, and the Psalms, and he showed that it was necessary for Christ to suffer.

Saul affirmed that nothing could supersede Moses. Stephen quoted Moses' words that the Lord God would raise up a greater prophet than himself.

All this Stephen declared with the greatest reverence and awe. How little he realized that the seed he dropped into the heart of his chief opponent would bear harvests to many millions throughout the centuries in the broad harvest field of the world!

The verbal battle rose and fell within the walls of that Cilician synagogue. It was an amazing conflict as ancient authority faced individual responsibility. It was the battle of all the ages in miniature, the one eternal conflict between form and spirit, between a false religiousness and the religion of the soul which stands unveiled before God.

Paul was powerfully affected by Stephen's death. That light on the martyr's face; that patience and forgiveness; that peace which surrounded his mangled body as he died—Paul could never forget them. He later molded his own great speeches on the model of that never-to-be-forgotten address.

The blood of the martyrs is the seed of the Church. The power of the persecutor is overcome by the patience of his victims. Saul, at whose feet witnesses lay down their outer cloaks, took up the mantle of the departing prophet and saint.

Chapter 3

ENCOUNTER ON THE ROAD

If the importance of events can be estimated by the amount of space given in Scripture to their narration, the arrest placed by the risen Lord upon Saul of Tarsus must take the second place in the New Testament. It is described three times with great detail—first by Luke and twice by Paul himself. The narration occupies more space than the story of any other event except the crucifixion of our Lord.

Paul knew without a doubt that he had seen the Lord. Therefore, he was as qualified to be a witness of His resurrection as Peter or John. "Am I not an apostle?...have I not seen Jesus Christ our Lord?" he asks in 1 Corinthians 9:1. He lists the Lord's appearances after His resurrection and adds, "Last of all he was seen of me also, of one born out of due time" (1 Corinthians 15:9).

Six days earlier, Saul had left Jerusalem with a small escort furnished by the high priest. The journey was long and lonely, giving him time for reflection. During the previous months, he had been on a rampage of trials, scourgings, and martyrdoms.

It was high noon on the Damascus Road. Unlike most travelers, Paul refused to spend even an hour in the retirement of his tent for shelter from the fierce rays of the sun. He was too eager to be at his work.

But suddenly a great light, brighter than the sun, shone around him. A voice amid the blaze, unintelligible to his companions spoke in Aramaic and called him by name. (See Acts 26:14.)

That light came straight from the face of the glorified Savior. In the glory of that light, Paul became convinced of the truth of Christianity. His objection to Christianity was not that Jesus of Nazareth had been crucified. Had this been all, the young Pharisee would have respected Him. His blameless life and sound teaching would have even attracted Paul's admiration. But it was intolerable that He should pose as the Messiah or that His followers should charge the rulers with the murder of the long-expected King.

Only one thing could ever convince him. He must see this Jesus of Nazareth whom he knew had been crucified. He must be able to recognize and establish His identity and hear Him speak. Such evidence would be conclusive, and nothing less would satisfy him.

This precise revelation was made to him. He was too sane to base the entire change of his career upon a mere dream, vision, or hallucination. When he met

Jesus, he knew instantly that life must have a new meaning and purpose. He would now live to establish the faith that he had attempted to destroy.

In the glory of that light, Paul received the supreme revelation of God. No conceivable method of divine manifestation can exceed the light that shines from the face of Jesus. Human features looked down on the persecutor through the open doorway of heaven; but they were aglow with the light of that Shekinah which, at the dedication of Solomon's Temple, drove the priests before its waves of glory from the holy place into the outer court. He beheld the glory of God in the face of Jesus whom he had persecuted.

In the revelation of that light, Saul of Tarsus saw the true nature of the war he had been waging against the Church of Jesus. He had devastated the believers with the fury of an invading army. Not content with attacks on their public meetings, he visited their homes, dragging out the women as well as the men, scourging them, thrusting them in prison, putting them to death, and compelling them to blaspheme the holy name by which they were called. He breathed out threats and slaughter. When the Church at Jerusalem at last lay desolate, he pursued the believers to the distant cities where they had fled. He had even received letters to arrest those of the Way in Damascus and bring them to Jerusalem to be punished.

Although his tender nature must have revolted from his ruthless efforts, he pursued the believers with the enthusiastic encouragement of his fellow religious leaders. There was, however, a deeper motive at work. This work of extermination was part of his religious duty. He owed it to God to stamp out the followers of Jesus. Like the Roman soldiers who crucified the the Lord, he did not realize what he did. He later admitted to being "a blasphemer, and a persecutor, and injurious: but I obtained mercy, because I did it ignorantly in unbelief" (1 Timothy 1:13).

As that light fell from heaven upon Paul's path, he suddenly discovered that instead of serving God, he was uprooting and ravaging the purpose for which His Son had expended tears and blood. In persecuting the sect of the Nazarenes, he was persecuting the Son of God. Instead of his fanatical zeal being pleasing to God, it was grievous to Him. It is an awful discovery when a great light from heaven shows a man that what he has regarded as his solemn duty has been instead sin against God.

When the Master said, "It is hard for thee to kick against the pricks" (Acts 9:5), His words also revealed His identity. During His earthly ministry, Jesus spoke to His people in parables. This time He likened Himself to one who had purchased a young heifer at a great price. He brought it into the field to plow in a certain direction; but it resisted, compelling its owner to use the sharply-pointed goad pressed against its flanks. Saul realized that he had been purchased by the Lord, who had been seeking for a long time to get him to follow the Way. From this time on, he was not to do his own will but God's.

Saul meekly asked what the new and rightful Master of his life would have him do. How could he be other than obedient to the heavenly vision that summoned him to a life of self-sacrificing toil?

Chapter 4

BEGINNING THE CHRISTIAN LIFE

Saul's entrance into Damascus was much different than he had anticipated. During his weary six-day journey, he looked forward to his reception as the commissioner of the high priest.

But instead of honor, Paul was met with consternation and surprise. Instead of the haughty bearing of an inquisitor, he came as a helpless, sightless man, appealing for someone to lead him. Shrinking from notice and welcome, he was eager to reach a lonely room where he could recover from the awful effects of that collision between his sinful nature and the holy, glorious Son of God whom he had ruthlessly persecuted.

"It pleased God...to reveal his Son in me" (Galatians 1:15-16). Paul knew too much of the divine life to admit that the vast change in him could be entirely accounted for by what he had seen with his now blinded eyes. He was aware that a true and lasting work can only be achieved when the spiritual eye has perceived things that are hidden from the physical senses. God, who commanded the light to shine out of darkness, must shine in the heart to give the light of the knowledge of His glory in the face of Jesus. (See 2 Corinthians 4:6.)

Imagine the abundance of revelations made to the blinded man during those three days and nights of silence and solitude in the house of a man named Judas. (See Acts 9:11.) During those wondrous hours, God unveiled secrets hidden through eternity to Paul that he might make them known to all nations.

But the crowning revelation of all was the unveiling of Christ living within him by His Spirit. Paul was in Christ, and Christ was in him, just as the branch has its place in the vine, and the vine lives through the branch.

God trusted Ananias with the keys of the Kingdom so that he might unlock Saul's way into perfect peace. We know little of Ananias except that he was a devout man according to the law and was evidently on intimate terms with his Master. The Lord reassured him of His plan before sending him forth to lay hands upon Saul.

Ananias gave Saul a brother's welcome. Although he was fully acquainted with the reason of Saul's visit to the city, he greeted him with the sweet words, *"Brother* Saul" (Acts 9:17). What a thrill that address sent through the heart of the new convert! None of the Pharisees ever spoke like this. As Paul became conscious of the presence of this new brother standing beside him and laying his hand on his fevered brow, the human love was the sign and symbol of the divine.

He communicated priceless blessings. First, through the laying on of his hands, sight returned to Paul's eyes. Ananias' touch, accompanied as it must have been with prayer and faith, was also the signal for Paul to receive the anointing grace of the Holy Spirit.

Ananias also baptized Paul. What a baptism that must have been! A tidal wave of emotion must have swept over Paul as he realized that he was being united with Jesus by the likeness of His death! Baptism was his final and irreversible break with his past life, the Pharisaic party, and his persecution of the Christians. From that moment he took up his cross and began to follow his Master.

It does not appear that Ananias knew all that baptism meant to his new brother, Saul. To him it was an act of obedience, a symbol of the washing away of sins. This simple soul had never trodden the difficult way of the cross. His help must have been comforting to the new disciple as he united himself with the cross of Jesus. All Ananias knew was that the Lord had said, "I will shew him how great things he must suffer for my name's sake" (Acts 9:16).

Paul tells us of the days following his conversion: "Immediately I conferred not with flesh and blood: Neither went I up to Jerusalem to them which were apostles before me; but I went away into Arabia" (Galatians 1:16-17). It is not clear whether Paul began to preach before going, but he probably did not. He wanted to be alone to reflect on all that he had seen and coordinate, if possible, the new with the old and the present with the past. For this reason, he hungered for the isolation and solitude of the wilderness.

Men like Ananias might reassure him; the apostles of the Lord might help him prepare for his wondrous ministry; the beauty of life in the infant Church might calm and elevate his spirit; but, above all things, he wanted to be alone with Jesus, to know Him and the power of His resurrection. The anointing of the Holy Spirit makes human teaching unnecessary because it teaches all things. Three years under such training made Paul so well-versed in the faith that when he met the other apostles, they would need to add nothing to his understanding.

How much it must have meant to Paul's eager spirit to finally understand the inner meaning of the momentous events of Jewish history which had taken place in the mountain solitudes! Here the bush had burned with the fire that now burned within his heart. Here Moses had seen God face to face, as he had seen Jesus. Here the plan of the tabernacle had been communicated, as he received the plan for the Church. Here the water flowed from the rock, and that Rock was Christ. Here Elijah stood in the entrance to the cave, when the still, small voice stole into his heart. Now, Paul heard that same voice!

Paul's most important work of those years was to review the entire volume of Old Testament truth from the new standpoint of vision suggested by the suffering and death of the Messiah. The death and resurrection of Christ was consistent with the words of the prophets of the Old Testament.

Generations of rabbis used the prophecies to predict an all-victorious Prince. Now, Paul eagerly turned to all the well-known Messianic passages. What ecstasy must have thrilled him as he discovered that they were all consistent with Christ's suffering and death as the way to enter His glory! He must have wondered how he and his people had been so blind to the obvious meaning of the inspired Word.

After returning to Damascus, Paul immediately proclaimed that Jesus was the Son of God and the Messiah. In those silent meditations over the Word, he stored arguments for use in many synagogues for the next twenty years. But deeper than anything was God's work with his soul. Grain by grain, his proud self-reliance was worn away. No longer confident in himself, he became content to be the slave of Jesus Christ, going where he was sent, doing as he was told, and serving as the instrument of His will.

We all need to spend time alone with God to learn lessons like these. The Lord Himself was led up into the wilderness. In one form or another, every soul who has done a great work in the world has passed through similar periods of obscurity, suffering, or solitude.

Chapter 5

FINDING HIS PLACE

Often at the beginning of our new spiritual life, we attempt to forecast the work we hope to accomplish. We take into account our tastes, abilities, and circumstances. From these we infer that we will probably succeed best along a certain line of useful activity. But as the moments lengthen into years, the door of opportunity may close in that direction.

Only after such a period of disappointment can we understand that God's ways are not our ways, nor His thoughts our thoughts. (See Isaiah 55:8.) He has other work for us to do, and He has been preparing us, although we did not know it.

At the beginning of his Christian life, Paul felt strongly drawn to minister to his own people. What was the meaning of his birth and education in the heart of Judaism, except that he might better understand and win Jews to Christ? But he was destined to discover that his new Master had other purposes for him. He had been prepared and called to preach among the Gentiles.

When he returned to Damascus, Paul immediately began his crusade in the synagogues. "Straightway he preached Christ in the synagogues, that he is the Son of God. But all that heard him were amazed....But Saul increased the more in strength, and confounded the Jews which dwelt at Damascus, proving that this is the very Christ" (Acts 8:20-22).

How encouraged he was by these early successes! Visions of national repentance and conversion passed across his eager soul. He dared to hope that he would live to see the dry bones of the Hebrew people become a great army for God. (See Ezekiel 37:1-14.)

But the vision was soon clouded by the violent hatred of his countrymen. His life was in danger, and he had to be lowered in a basket over the city wall at night to escape.

Still, Paul's purpose was unchanged. He went up to Jerusalem with the intention of seeing Peter. But in this he probably would have failed had it not been for the intervention of Barnabas who brought him into contact with the believers in that city.

But Paul had other business in those days. He avoided the churches in Judea and again preached in the synagogues. "He spake boldly in the name of the Lord Jesus, and disputed against the Grecians." But here also his efforts were met by rebuffs. "They went about to slay him" (Acts 9:29).

In spite of their rejection, he clung tenaciously to his cherished purpose. In a similar manner we have all cherished our supposed life purpose. Not until long years have passed do we realize that the Lord's plan was much wiser and grander than our own.

The door had begun to close at Damascus. It closed further when persecution arose at Jerusalem. But the final act was as Saul was praying in the temple. He had gone there to be alone, away from the many voices that were attempting to counsel him. Although he had been in the city only a few days, opposition against him had already risen to such a height that his life was in danger. Some advised him to stay in the city, and others warned him to leave at once. The babble of voices confused him, deafening the whisper of the still, small voice of God.

He fled to the temple to be alone. As he knelt in prayer, the risen Lord gave clear and unmistakable directions, as He always will to those who wait before Him. "Make haste, and get thee quickly out of Jerusalem: for they will not receive thy testimony concerning me" (Acts 22:18).

It is easy to explain why they would not accept his testimony. There was too much of the cross in it. It wounded their pride to learn that the carpenter was the long-anticipated Messiah. Furthermore, the thought that true life could only be entered by death to oneself was intolerable.

Saul did not willingly accept their rejection as final. He still argued that Jerusalem would be the best place for his ministry. But all debate was at last closed by the words, "Depart: for I will send thee far hence unto the Gentiles" (Acts 22:21.)

The disciples brought the hunted preacher down to Caesarea and sent him to Tarsus. There Paul resumed his tent making, content to await the Lord's will and timing. But the years passed slowly. Possibly four or five were spent in comparative obscurity and neglect.

At last one day he heard a voice saying, "Does Saul live here?" In another moment the familiar face of his old friend Barnabas was peering in on him with a glad smile. He told Paul of the marvelous outbreak of God's work in Antioch. Barnabas pleaded with him to return to help him gather in the harvest of the first great Gentile city to receive the gospel. "He brought him to Antioch. And it came to pass, that a whole year they assembled themselves with the church, and taught much people" (Acts 11:26).

The year's experience at Antioch had a great effect on Paul. Barnabas told him about the decision of the Church at Jerusalem concerning God's dealings with Cornelius and his household. (See Acts 10:44-45; 11:18.) The Spirit of God set His anointing upon the preaching of the gospel directly to the Gentiles. Paul saw that believing Gentiles were fellow-members of the Church and fellow-heirs of the promises. God made no distinctions; why should he? His horizon was broadening, his confidence increasing, and his conception of God's purposes deepening.

Paul made a brief visit to Jerusalem at the end of his year's ministry at Antioch. He brought money with him from the Gentile Christians to help their suffering Jewish brethren. His action proved that there was no antagonism between the new society and the old but that all were one in Christ.

When Barnabas and Paul returned from Jerusalem, they met with three others for a time of fasting and prayer. This was the birth hour of modern missions. The Holy Spirit told them to set apart two out of their number to a mission that He would unfold to them as they dared to step out in obedience to His command. There was no hesitation or delay. The Church set Barnabas and Paul free from their duties, and the Holy Spirit sent them forth.

Cyprus was their first stop. Although they proclaimed the Word of God from one end of the island to the other in the synagogues of the Jews, they had no fruit. At last, the Roman governor called them before him to hear their message, and he believed. (See Acts 13:7-12.)

Then they sailed to the mainland to preach in the city of Perga. Paul left the seacoast for the tablelands of the interior, four thousand feet above sea level. He evidently intended to establish churches on the great trade route which ran through Asia Minor from Tarsus to Ephesus. Here, young John Mark deserted them and returned home.

The Jews in Antioch and Pisidia refused the gospel, but the Gentiles welcomed them. Paul was compelled to turn from his own countrymen and hold up the gospel as light and salvation to the Gentiles. The Word of the Lord quickly spread throughout the region.

The missionaries fled before a persecution incited

by the Jews which made it unsafe to remain in Antioch, and they came to Iconium. Again they found the malice of the Jews so persistent that they were driven into the district of Lycaonia, where there were probably no synagogues at all. There, too, they preached the gospel and made many disciples.

Everywhere they went, the Jews obstructed their ministry, while the Gentiles received them and their message with open arms. As Paul quietly studied these indications of God's will, he needed no angel to tell him that since Israel would not hear, God was provoking them to jealousy by working among the Gentiles. He saw that the original branches were being broken off so that the wild olive grafts might take their place. His love for his kinsmen was not diminished, but he knew that he must follow the divine plan.

James, Peter, and John realized that their former persecutor had received a divine commission to the Gentiles. The responsible leaders of the mother Church could not help perceiving the grace that was given to him. Finally, they gave him their support that he should go to the Gentiles while they would continue to try to reach the Jews.

This was the further and final confirmation of the purpose which had been forming in Paul's heart. He recognized that he was appointed to be a teacher of the Gentiles in faith and truth. He rejoiced in this ministry and often spoke of the grace which had been given to him, the least of all saints, to preach the unsearchable riches of Christ to the Gentiles.

Chapter 6

THE VISION AND THE THORN

Paul draws aside the veil from his heart and shares his inner experiences during those wonderful months as a missionary. He was a man in Christ, caught up into Paradise, the third heaven, to hear unspeakable words. (See 2 Corinthians 12:2-4.)

"A man in Christ"—Paul was in Christ, and that made him fulfilled as a man. Three qualities blend together to form a strong Christian character: resolution, fortitude, and courage.

Resolution causes a man to take up one high ambition and remain determined in it through good times and bad. Paul pursued his purpose of ministering to the Gentiles from Antioch to Iconium, and then to Lystra and Derbe. The hatred of the Jews, the fickleness of the crowds, and the stoning at Lystra did not turn him aside.

Fortitude helps man sustain sorrow and heart-rending anguish and then dare to praise God. Paul manifested this quality when he bore with the relentless hatred of his countrymen. After his stoning at

223

Lystra, he arose from what appeared to be his death and struggled back into the city from which he had been expelled. After greeting the brethren, and especially young Timothy, he started on the following morning to continue his work in the neighboring cities of Lycaonia.

Courage is a quality that Paul never lacked. He never flinched from facing an amphitheater full of raging fanatics, hostile government officials, or an apostle who needed correction. His heroic courage was manifested in this first missionary journey. Instead of taking the easy and direct route home by way of his native city, he dared to retrace his steps in each of the cities he had preached. At great personal risk, he stayed long enough in each place to appoint elders in the infant churches and to pray with fasting, commending them to God on whom they believed.

When we become Christians, we do not forfeit these characteristics. Rather, they become purified of ingredients that might corrupt them. Apart from Christ, resolution may become obstinancy, fortitude may become stoicism, and courage may become fatalism. These are exaggerations and, therefore, defects. The strength of Christian character is invigorated from the Lion of the tribe of Judah and sweetened by the meekness and gentleness of the Lamb who was slain.

''How that he was caught up into paradise, and heard unspeakable words, which it is not lawful for a man to utter. Of such an one will I glory'' (2 Corinthians 12:4-5). At first we might suppose that Paul was describing the experience of someone else. He appears to distinguish between that blessed man, whose experience he was describing, and himself. "Yet of myself I will not glory, but in my infirmities" (2 Corinthians 12:5). Because of the visions and revelations granted to him, he was in danger of being lifted up in pride. It becomes clear that he is describing some radiant experience through which he passed during that first missionary tour.

Glimpses into glory are as fleeting as they are unspeakable. We must not live in an experience but in Jesus. We must not get out of touch with the men and women around us. The majority of people do not live on mountain tops but in valleys where demons possess and worry the afflicted. Be content to turn, as Jesus did, from the rapture of Paradise on the Transfiguration Mount to take the way of the cross.

Paul enjoyed glorious experiences, but he also had to deal with the troublesome thorn in the flesh. While the nature of Paul's thorn is uncertain, it was definitely very painful. In infinite wisdom, God permitted the messenger of Satan to buffet His servant. All through that first missionary journey, Paul had to face a long succession of buffetings. There were perils of robbers, of waters, of mountain passes, and of violent crowds; but in addition to all, there was the lacerating thorn.

He asked the Lord on three separate occasions for deliverance and received the assurance that more than sufficient grace would be given. God's grace is sufficient when friends forsake and foes pursue. It can make His servant strong against a raging synagogue or a shower of stones and is sufficient for excessive labors of body and conflicts of soul. His grace is sufficient to cause His servant to do as much work, and even more, than if the body were perfectly whole—for strength is made perfect only amid the conditions of mortal weakness.

Our appreciation of Paul's work increases when we remember that he often suffered extreme discomfort. He did not sit down in despair and plead weakness as his excuse for doing nothing. Instead, he bravely claimed the grace and did greater work through God's enabling might than he could have done through his own had it been unhindered by his weakness.

Disabilities were meant to unite you with God's ability. God's sufficient grace is at its best when human weakness is most profound. Claim it, and learn that those who wait on God are stronger in their weakness than the sons of men in the best of health.

Paul needed the grace of God to overcome the next controversy that was about to erupt. In the epistle to the Galatians, we have a glimpse of the liberty which the converts in Antioch had in Christ Jesus. Circumcised and uncircumcised believers joined together in Christian fellowship.

The conservative party in the Jerusalem church, however, was ill at ease with this new freedom. They saw that if this principle were allowed to be universal, it would undermine their authority and eventually rend their religious supremacy from their grasp. Therefore, they sent false brethren to investigate the liberty which the church at Antioch practiced. Then, when they were assured of the facts, certain men came from Judea and taught the brethren, saying, "Except ye be circumcised after the manner of Moses, ye cannot be saved" (Acts 15:1). This crisis led to the breaking out of a controversy which embittered many years in Paul's life. But it also led to some of his most noble epistles and to his exposition of the principles of the gospel with clarity and beauty.

The conditions of salvation are debated in every age. The terms vary, but the controversy is always the same. Men still say, "Unless you are christened, confirmed, and received into our church, you cannot be saved."

Salvation is not secured by obedience to a rite, by the observance of a code of rules, or even by obedience to a creed which is pronounced orthodox. A man may be precise in all of these and yet be under the wrath of God. The only condition of salvation is believing faith that justifies the ungodly. This faith receives into the heart the nature of Jesus to become the power of the new life.

People tend to magnify the importance of religious rites and minimize the value of the spiritual attribute. The outward is much more manageable and measurable. The spiritual is beyond human vision and manipulation. In these days men magnify the ordinances of baptism and the Lord's Supper in the same way these Judaizing Christians magnified circumcision. When he is allowed to do so, man's religion becomes mechanical and formal.

The disputing and questioning showed no signs of abating. Paul, Barnabas, and certain others were sent up to Jerusalem to consult the apostles and elders about the importance of circumcision. They traveled slowly through Phoenicia and Samaria, sharing the news of the conversion of the Gentiles in each of the little Christian communities on their route. At last, they reached Jerusalem. There, in a great missionary convocation, they told all the things that God had done with them.

The Pharisaic party was defeated, but from that moment a relentless war broke out which followed Paul for the next ten years of his life and cost him many bitter tears. Every church he planted was visited by his opponents who were no longer content with insisting on the necessity of circumcision. They further asserted that Paul was not an apostle because he had only seen Christ in a vision. They maligned his personal character, misrepresented his reluctance to take the gifts of his converts, dwelt with cruel animosity upon his personal defects, and in many cases succeeded in alienating the love and loyalty of his converts.

This cruel persecution is constantly alluded to in the letters to the Galatians and Corinthians, and it cut Paul to the heart. But he never was defeated. By prayers, tears, arguments, and persuasions, he fought the good fight to the end. From the tone of his later epistles, it sounds as if he was permitted to see the close of the controversy. It was finally agreed that the new-wine Christianity should not be poured into the worn-out wineskins of Judaism.

Chapter 7

THE SECOND JOURNEY

After a period of preaching and teaching in Antioch, Paul proposed to Barnabas that they visit the brethren in every city where they had proclaimed the Word of the Lord. This was the beginning of his second missionary journey that was to have far-reaching results.

Barnabas suggested that they take John Mark with them as before, a proposition which Paul refused to consider. John Mark had deserted them on the threshold of their previous expedition, and Paul was concerned that he might do so again. The church became aware of their disagreement and took Paul's side. The narrative of Acts tells us that Paul chose Silas and went forth, "recommended by the brethren unto the grace of God" (Acts 15:40).

When we are about to undertake some great venture for God, Satan often attempts to overthrow us through conflict with our associates. Nothing tests us more than this. It is difficult to be both resolute and gentle, strong and sweet. If you are compelled to disagree with your companions, let it be done in love. Let them know that you have no interests to serve but those of truth. Perfect love is the only atmosphere in which the divine Spirit can manifest His gracious help.

Through regions rich in flowers and natural beauty, Paul and Silas traversed Syria and Cilicia, strengthening the infant churches which probably owed their existence to Paul's earliest efforts. They went on to Tarsus, but there was no welcome for them there. During their days of toilsome travel, they visited Derbe, Lystra, and Iconium.

What a welcome Paul received in these cities! There was, however, a special burden on the apostle's heart. He asked about Timothy and was glad to learn that the young convert had been faithful to the teachings of those who had instructed him in the Holy Scriptures.

Paul proposed that Timothy accompany him on his travels as his own son in the faith. He administered the rite of circumcision as a matter of convenience, so that there might be no obstacle to the admission of his young assistant to Jewish synagogues. (See Acts 16:3.)

A simple ordination service was then held, and Timothy was solemnly set apart for his great work. The elders gathered around, laid their hands on his bowed head, and prayed. Thus the Spirit of Jesus called a new laborer into the harvest field and endowed him with special qualifications for the work.

Leaving Lystra, Paul and his companions visited

the churches in Phyrgia and Galatia, distributing the letter of James. They planned to go into the large and influential cities of Asia Minor, such as Colossae, Laodicea, and Ephesus. But they "were forbidden of the Holy Ghost to preach the word in Asia" (Acts 16:6).

Paul would later do some of the greatest work of his life in that region; but now the door was closed against him by the Holy Spirit. The time was not yet ripe for the attack on these apparently impregnable bastions of the kingdom of Satan.

The travelers, therefore, took a northern route, with the intention of entering the province of Bithynia along the shores of the Black Sea. But when they attempted to go out of Asia Minor into Bithynia, the Spirit of Jesus did not permit them. They could only go straight until they came to the end of the road at the famous harbor of Troas. There, in a night vision, a man of Macedonia beckoned the missionaries to set up the banner of Christ on the continent of Europe.

All believers should study the method of the Holy Spirit's guidance of these early heralds of the gospel. When they tried to turn to Asia, He stopped them; and when they sought to enter Bithynia, He prevented them again. He shut all the doors along their route except for the one He wanted them to walk through. They had no alternative but to go forward.

Whenever you are doubtful about your course, submit your judgment to the Spirit of God and ask

Him to shut every door but the right one. Meanwhile, continue along the path you have been already treading. Keep going on as you are, unless you are clearly told to do something else. Expect to have as clear a door out as you had in. Consider the absence of His indication to be the evidence of God's will that you are on His track.

Paul continued his journey, content to go wherever the Spirit led him. Along the way, he drew many men and women to himself. In Philippi, he won a group of friends who never ceased to love him. When other disciples became alienated and weary, they remained true. Whatever trouble threatened to engulf him, it only brought their greater help.

Luke, the beloved physician, first met Paul at Troas. Here in all likelihood, the servant of God won his medical attendant for the Savior. In the enthusiasm of their newly formed spiritual bond and friendship, the new disciple elected to become his fellow-traveler.

How dear Luke became to the apostle! Their close friendship is evident in two expressions penned by Paul: one from the house of his first Roman imprisonment and the other from a cold prison cell. "Luke, the beloved physician"; "Only Luke is with me" (Colossians 4:14, 2 Timothy 4:11).

Lydia was probably a widow of considerable business ability. She left her native city of Thyatira and crossed the sea to establish herself in Philippi as agent for the sale of purple-dyed garments. She must have possessed a considerable amount of capital to be able to deal in these expensive articles. She was also an eager seeker after God.

The Jewish community at Philippi, too small and poor to have a synagogue of its own, was obliged to meet by the riverside. One memorable Sabbath, four Jewish strangers appeared in the little circle. They "sat down and spake unto the women which resorted thither" (Acts 16:13). This was the first gospel sermon preached in Europe.

The result of that morning service was that Lydia, with her entire household, came to believe in Jesus. She eagerly told Paul and his companions, "If ye have judged me to be faithful unto the Lord, come into my house, and abide there" (Acts 16:15).

She must have been a woman of considerable determination and perseverance to have overcome Paul's reluctance to be dependent on any of his converts. He would bear anything rather than risk the suspicion that he was making a profit out of the gospel. But Lydia was able to override all his objections, and the four companions in travel found a place of rest in her home. On four separate occasions in later years, the Philippian church sent supplies to their beloved founder and teacher. This was probably due to Lydia's foresight and generosity.

Paul met another of his faithful friends in a Philippian jail. The jailer was a rough, coarse man. What else could be expected from one who had spent his early days in the Roman army and his later ones amid the brutalizing experiences of a Roman prison? The inner prison was a dark, underground hole beneath his house, and into this he thrust Paul and Silas. They were left on the bare, damp ground, their bleeding backs in contact with the soil, and their legs stretched to such an extent by the stocks as to almost dislocate their hips.

By midnight, the two prisoners became filled with the joy of the Lord, and they began to sing and pray. It was an unusual sound to the other prisoners who lay in the pitch dark, their chains fastened to the walls.

Suddenly, an earthquake broke in on the singing, the doors flew open, and the chains fell off. The jailer, being roused from sleep, came into the prison yard and found the doors open. Paul and Silas caught sight of him standing against the glimmering starlight. To their horror, they saw him draw his sword and prepare to kill himself rather than face death for allowing prisoners to escape.

Paul shouted and reassured him that all of the prisoners were still there. The trembling jailer entered the cell and asked, ''Sirs, what must I do to be saved?'' That night, he believed on the Lord Jesus Christ and was saved, along with his whole household.

The jailer became one of the members of the Philippian church, a community of purity and love. To them the apostle wrote his tenderest words without a syllable of rebuke.

Chapter 8

ADVENTURES IN PREACHING

Leaving Luke at Philippi, Paul and his companions traveled to Thessalonica, a name which lives forever in the inscriptions of his two earliest epistles. He remained there long enough to allow the formation of a healthy and vigorous church. Paul later spoke of these Macedonian converts as his joy and crown. They were very poor, and Paul worked day and night that he might not be a burden to them; but they were rich in faith, love, and hope. (See 1 Thessalonians 2:6-9.)

Paul must have been occupied for several months in this blessed ministry. The strain on the apostle was reduced by the gifts which came from Philippi, relieving him from the necessity of manual labor. (See Philippians 4:16.)

At last, the open door for ministry in Thessalonica was closed against them. Paul and Silas were compelled to flee by night before the anger of the citizens, incited by the Jews. Fifty miles of night journey brought them to Berea. They rejoiced when they found that those Jews were willing to search the Scriptures to discover for themselves the truth concerning the gospel. But Paul's heart yearned for the beloved brethren in Thessalonica.

Paul's return was, however, rendered quite impossible by the rising of another storm. Jewish emissaries from Thessalonica pursued him with relentless hate. At last no choice remained but to leave Silas and Timothy in Berea and to hurry down to the harbor to take the first boat that was sailing. This happened to be bound for Athens. We can imagine Paul standing on deck, watching wistfully as the receding heights of Mount Olympus slowly faded from view. He was leaving behind the dearest, truest friends he had ever known.

The messengers hastened back to Berea, bearing the charge of the lonely apostle that Silas and Timothy should come to him as soon as possible. Meanwhile, Paul arrived in Athens. He passed through the streets, surveying the monuments of their religion. On every side stood the achievements of human genius.

To Paul, however, the city was simply full of idols; and the large number of them suggested the confused notions that prevailed of the unity and majesty of God. Not content with preaching in the synagogue to the Jews and proselytes, he went forth every day into the marketplace to reason with whomever he met, urging them to turn from these vanities to worship the only God. The townsmen finally took hold of him and brought him before their highest religious tribunal.

It was the greatest audience Paul had ever addressed. Before him stood philosophers, lecturers, and students accustomed to discussing the loftiest themes within the horizon of human thought. Epicureans were there to taste the flow of words and criticize the style of the message. Stoics came to study the theory of life which this new theorizer professed. The whole crowd of Athenians and visitors were interested only in hearing something new.

The address Paul gave on that occasion is quite unique. In its grace and intellectual sequence, it stands alone among the addresses recorded for us by the evangelist. It was probably the result of deep thought and prayer, or Paul would not have so carefully passed it to Luke, who was not then with him. It reveals Paul's ability to relate to all sorts and conditions of men. But when Paul mentioned the resurrection of Jesus the Messiah, many in his audience began to mock him. He was forced to depart with comparatively little success.

As far as we know, Paul never visited Athens again. He went sadly on his way to Corinth, his heart filled with a tumult of thoughts, anxious for the infant churches behind him. He longed to see Timothy and Luke, wondering what reception he would get from the cultured and eloquent Corinthians.

Five hours' sail across the Saronic Bay brought Paul to Cenchrea, the port of Corinth to the east.

This great and busy city commanded two waterways. To establish a strong Christian church there would be to cast seeds of Christian teaching on waters that would bear them east and west.

But the apostle entered the proud and beautiful city "in weakness, and fear, and much trembling" (1 Corinthians 2:3). He could not forget the contempt he had encountered at Athens, which was harder to bear than violent opposition. Many difficulties waited to be faced, which made his ministry in Corinth difficult and his success obviously due to the power of God.

Paul maintained the right of those who preached the gospel to make their living by the gospel. But he did not so that the merchants and traders that thronged the city could not allege that he was motivated by personal gain. He, therefore, resumed his trade of tent making. He was thankful to meet two Christian Jews, Aquila and his wife Priscilla who also worked at the same trade. They had arrived on this shore by the decree of the Emperor which expelled all Jews from Rome. With them, Paul lived and worked, and a friendship grew between them which influenced the spread of Christianity in Rome and Ephesus.

According to his usual practice, Paul spent every Sabbath in the synagogue, persuading the Jews and Greek proselytes that the Hebrew Scriptures clearly point to a suffering and crucified Messiah. This went on for some weeks; but his labors were curtailed by the heavy drain of his daily toil. Finally, Timothy arrived from Thessalonica and Silas returned from Berea. They brought encouraging news of the steadfastness of his converts, and their hands were full of generous gifts. Now that he had more time for preaching, Paul "was pressed in the spirit, and testified to the Jews that Jesus was Christ" (Acts 18:5).

This was more than the influential men of the Jewish community could bear. They drove him from the synagogue. Their hatred culminated when Paul gladly accepted the offer of a God-fearing proselyte, Titus Justus, to hold meetings in his home near the synagogue. This new move was accompanied with instant and remarkable success. Among those that left with the apostle from the synagogue was Crispus, its chief ruler, who believed in the Lord with all his house. Many of the people of Corinth also heard, believed, and were baptized.

As the new meetinghouse became more crowded, and the movement increased in numbers and influence, the Jews became more and more exasperated. At last they seized Paul and dragged him before the Roman governor. The governor represented the broad and liberal views of educated Romans. When he discovered that the charge against Paul had nothing to do with civil wrong or moral outrage but with words, names, and Jewish law, he would have nothing more to do with them. He commanded his officials to drive them from the court.

Paul was free to continue preaching. But the incident greatly aggravated the hatred of the Jews against the apostle and his converts. Furthermore, many of these converts came from the lower classes of this impure city. Soldiers, sailors, slaves, prostitutes, and athletes were looking for business or amusement in Corinth. The Temple of Venus, with its thousand priestesses, legalized vice. The Isthmian Games, held once in three years, established betting and gambling. The motley character of the population encouraged a wild mixture of thought and opinion with no recognized standard or court of appeal.

To such a city Paul opened his message, encouraged by the assurance of the Lord: "Be not afraid, but speak, and hold not thy peace: For I am with thee, and no man shall set on thee to hurt thee: for I have much people in this city" (Acts 18:9-10).

With this encouragement in his heart, Paul labored for a year and six months in this sinful city with marvelous success. The majority of his converts, however, were of the lowest class who had been deeply stained with the vices that made Corinth notorious. The city was the resort of fornicators, idolaters, adulterers, homosexuals, thieves, drunkards, revilers, and extortioners. But under the preaching of the gospel, in the power of the Holy Spirit, a marvelous change had taken place in them—they had become washed, sanctified, and justified in the name of the Lord Jesus and in the Spirit of God. Delivered from the power of darkness, they had become children of the light.

But the apostle was far from satisfied. He complained that he could not speak to them as spiritual men but as babes in Christ. He was obliged to feed them with milk and not with meat, and he detected the first working of the strife that would later break out. Even before he left, there were manifestations of a party spirit and the mistaking of license for liberty. He saw the undue prominence of women in public assemblies, greed in the love feasts, confusion in the gifts, and heresy in the doctrine of the resurrection. With great reluctance, he tore himself away at the close of his sojourn, leaving the infant community in the care of God.

Many reasons prompted this step, and among them was the desire to proceed to Jerusalem to meet with the mother church. Aquila and Priscilla thought that Ephesus would provide a better market for their wares than Corinth, so they sailed with him.

Thus the first memorable missionary tour in Greece came to an end. For the fourth time since his conversion, the apostle approached the city that was doubly dear to him—memories of his Lord were now entwined with the sacred associations of David, Solomon, Hezekiah, and Ezra.

Chapter 9

MORE THAN A CONQUEROR

Paul greeted the church in Jerusalem, then he went to visit the brethren in Syrian Antioch. But his eager spirit was unable to rest amid the comparative comfort and ease of the vigorous church life. He yearned to see his converts in Galatia and Phrygia.

He, therefore, again passed through the Cilician Gates and traversed the bleak tablelands of the upper country, encouraging all the disciples while heading toward the Roman province of Asia. He had been previously forbidden by the Holy Spirit to enter this region. (See Acts 16:6.) But now his steps were as clearly led to it as they had formerly been restrained.

Our sovereign Lord may withhold from His servants the immediate fulfillment of their dreams, so that they may return to them again when the time is ripe and they are more thoroughly equipped. The experiences of Paul in Greece prepared him for his ministry in this thickly-populated and highly-civilized district. His work of evangelization resulted in the formation of the seven churches to which the risen Lord addressed His final messages. (See Revelation 2-3.)

Paul at last came to Ephesus. He had spent one Sabbath day there on his way from Corinth to Jerusalem. His message deeply interested the Jews, and they had urged him to stay. But Paul was hurrying to Jerusalem to fulfill his vow. He promised them, "I will return again unto you, if God will" (Acts 18:21).

A good deal had happened in the meantime. Apollos, the eloquent Alexandrian, had visited the city and met Paul's friends, Aquila and Priscilla. They led him into a clear understanding of the truth which caused his ministry to become more fruitful, both in edifying the believers and powerfully refuting the Jews. The strong plow had prepared the soil for Paul's further labors.

But Apollos had now left for Corinth, and Paul arrived to take up and extend the work. He probably didn't realize how long he would remain in Ephesus or the far-reaching results of his residence. He only knew that a prepared path awaited him.

Paul faced opposition from beginning to end. "I fought with beasts at Ephesus" (1 Corinthians 15:32), he commented later. He compared his experiences to a battle and himself to a soldier, crying, "We are killed all the day long; we are accounted as sheep for the slaughter. Nay, in all these things we are more than conquerors through him that loved us'' (Romans 8:37). In these words, written to Rome from Corinth after the close of his work at Ephesus, he gives his own view of the entire situation.

Paul endured the pressure of the strange group of people whose interests, aims, and methods of thought were foreign to his own. How could he hope to affect its habits of thought and life? He might as well attempt to divert the course of an ancient stream.

Besides, a vast system of organized idolatry centered around the temple of Diana. Her image was said to have fallen from Jupiter (possibly a meteorite), and it was enshrined in a temple, counted to be one of the wonders of the world. The magnificence of uncalculated wealth, the masterpieces of human art, the frame of splendid ceremonies, the lavish gifts of emperors and kings, the attendance and service of thousands of priests and priestesses—all combined to give it unrivaled influence and prestige.

In connection with the temple, the trade in amulets and charms flourished. Each individual in the vast crowds that came to worship at the shrine was eager to carry back some momento of his visit, hoping that the keepsake would protect against evil omens and spirits. It seemed impossible that one man, in three years, employing only moral and spiritual weapons, could make any difference to this ancient and extensive craft.

Furthermore, like·many of the cities of the time

filled with diverse populations—part Oriental and part Greek—Ephesus was deeply infected with the black arts of magic and the occult. Even the converts to Christianity found it hard to divest themselves of their former association with these practices. The people decided everything from wedding dates to business transactions after an appeal to the soothsayers and magicians. It was a formidable task to combat their rooted prejudices and habits.

But perhaps Paul's worst foe was the Jewish synagogue, entrenched in ancient prejudices and persistent disbelief. They were hardened and disobedient, speaking evil of "the Way" before the multitude.

These giant obstacles confronted the humble tent maker as he settled down to his trade with Aquila and Priscilla. But he looked far beyond the limits of his workshop to great victories for his Lord. In all these things, he was destined to be more than a conqueror through Him that had loved him.

After three month's conflict with the Jews in their synagogue, the apostle moved his disciples to the schoolhouse of Tyrannus where he taught daily. The silversmiths acknowledged that not only at Ephesus but throughout all Asia Paul had persuaded many people to turn to Christ. The temple was in danger of losing its worshippers, and Diana was nearly deposed from her magnificence. The trade in amulets and charms fell off seriously, and the craftsmen realized that unless they took action, their gains would be at an end. Therefore, they started a riot, hoping that Paul would be killed.

The magicians and exorcists were utterly baffled by the great miracles worked through Paul. Many of them believed and came confessing their deeds. They brought their books together in the open square and burned them in the sight of all. The Word of the Lord grew mightily and prevailed.

If we turn from Paul's outward life to study the diary of this wonderful man, we find a pathetic record of his sorrows and trials. Writing during these eventful months, he speaks of himself as a man doomed to death and made a spectacle to the world. For Christ's sake, he became a fool—weak, and dishonored. He suffered hunger and thirst when work was scant and ill paid. He was hated, buffeted, reviled, persecuted, and defamed. (See 1 Corinthians 4:9-13.)

When he tells the story of the affliction during his residence in Asia, he says that he was weighed down beyond his strength. He even despaired of life. He was pressed on every side, perplexed, pursued, and struck down. In addition to all these things, he was responsible for the care of all the churches. He was also concerned about individual converts as he continued to admonish every one of them night and day with tears. (See 2 Corinthians 1:8; 4:8-10; 11:27-28.)

Added to this was the constant suffering caused by the thorn in the flesh. How could such a man in the face of such opposing forces, be more than a conqueror? Evidently, the source of Paul's victory was outside himself. He not only overcame, but he was more than an overcomer. He overcame with ease because he was in daily communication with One who would love him without end.

Chapter 10

A PRISONER OF JESUS

After the great uproar at Ephesus was over, Paul sent for his disciples to come to his place of hiding. He exhorted them, commending them to the grace of God and saying a sad farewell. He then departed for Macedonia by way of Troas.

At Troas, the apostle expected to meet Titus who had probably carried the first letter to Corinth—a letter prompted by the sad story of the dissension and disorders of the church there. He had dealt severely with the situation and was anxious to learn the result of his words. Often since writing he had questioned whether he might have destroyed his influence for good over his converts and driven them into defiance and despair.

The delay of Titus confirmed his worst fears. Although a great door of ministry was opened at Troas, he could find no relief for his spirit. Leaving them he went into Macedonia. (See 2 Corinthians 2:13.)

But even there, since no news of Titus was available, his concerns had no relief. At last, God comforted him by the arrival of the overdue traveler. He was glad to have his friend at his side and to learn that his letter had led to godly repentance and affection for himself. After conferring with Titus on the state of affairs at Corinth, he wrote his second letter.

Paul's next journey from Troas, down the ragged shores of Asia Minor, was sadder to his little group of devoted followers than to Paul. He had no doubt as to its final outcome. He was heading to Jerusalem, sure that there, as in every other city, bonds and afflictions awaited him. Of this the Holy Spirit gave unequivocal testimony. He prolonged his last speech at Troas until midnight and sent for the elders of the Ephesian church to meet him at Miletus. He knew that they would never see him again. He said farewell to the little group who waved their good-byes across the waters to his receding ship.

The Spirit's words spoken through the disciples at Tyre only confirmed what He had said to the heart of Paul. (See Acts 20:23.) Agabus the prophet foretold in striking symbolism what had been predicted already by that inward Prophet whose voice cannot be bribed.

To those that loved Paul, the prophetic warnings of coming disaster were like the falling of dirt on a coffin of one's dearest friend. Luke gives us a pathetic picture of the scene in the house of Philip, their host at Caesarea. Agabus came from Jerusalem, bound himself with Paul's belt, and announced that in a like manner the Jews would bind its owner.

"And," says Luke, "when we heard these things, both we, and they of that place, besought him not to go up to Jerusalem" (Acts 21:12). They wept, nearly breaking Paul's heart. But he was ready not only to be bound but also to die at Jerusalem for the name of the Lord Jesus. His greatest desire was to fulfill the ministry which he had received—to testify the gospel of the grace of God.

Paul's trials and circumstances resulted in the furtherance of the gospel. They gave him an opportunity to manifest the traits of a true Christian character. In addition, he was able to proclaim his testimony for Jesus before the highest tribunal in the world.

First, there was the awful riot in the temple court. The Jews of Asia laid hold of Paul, under the impression that he had brought an Ephesian into the court reserved for Jews. They dragged him down the steps, furiously beating him, with the intent of murdering him when they reached the bottom. With great difficulty, he was rescued by Lysias and his soldiers. They had rushed down from the adjoining Castle of Antonia, surrounded him with their shields, and carried him back on their shoulders from the frenzied mob. In the midst of the tumult, Paul obtained permission to address the people, weaving the story of the risen Jesus ingeniously into his personal narrative, so that they had to listen.

The following day, he was arraigned before the Sanhedrin. Annas, who sat to judge him, had been deposed from the high priesthood by right, although he continued to exercise that office. Paul immediately brought up the question of the resurrection because it was the one point at issue between him and the Jews. The Pharisees professed to believe in the resurrection, and yet refused to admit that Jesus had risen. Paul, on the other hand, sought to establish not only that there would be a resurrection, but that there had been one already.

His efforts to use these trying scenes for the glory of his Master were abundantly rewarded by the vision of the Lord who said, "Be of good cheer, Paul: for as thou hast testified of me in Jerusalem, so must thou bear witness also at Rome" (Acts 23:11).

Paul's nephew, who was evidently trusted with the secret of his foes and must have passed as a bigoted Jew, risked being killed to warn Paul of the plot of the zealots. They had bound themselves by a solemn vow neither to eat nor drink until they had forever silenced the tongue that filled them with rage and fear.

Paul told the chief captain of his danger and was immediately hurried by soldiers in a forced march, by night, to Antipatris, thirty-five miles away. The next day, they journeyed twenty-five miles further to Caesarea, to undergo trial before Felix, the Roman governor of Judea. But, as usual, Paul seemed less eager to speak of himself and more determined to use every opportunity of his public position to reason with his judge concerning the faith in Christ Jesus. He spoke powerfully of righteousness, self-control, and judgment to come, in the presence of

Felix and the woman with whom he was living in adultery. Felix trembled as the prisoner compelled him to review a life of shame beneath the searchlight of an awakened conscience.

Two years later, Festus came to take the place of Felix, who had been recalled in disgrace. Within a few days, Paul greatly impressed the newcomer with his faith in Jesus. But perhaps Paul's greatest opportunity came when he was able to preach the gospel to an assembly that comprised all the fashion, wealth, and distinction of the land.

Festus was there, and the Herods, brother and sister, were seated on golden chairs. The officers of the garrison and the principal men of the city filled the room. How great a contrast between the splendid pomp of that occasion and the poor, chained prisoner at the bar! Yet although bending under the weight of sixty years and many sorrows, he was the noblest and fairest of all the glittering throng. How grandly he preached Christ that day as he made his defense! He told the story of the suffering and risen Lord and the fulfillment of the predictions of Moses and the prophets. The turning from darkness to light and the conditions of forgiven sin and an inheritance among the saints were recited with passionate earnestness. The Roman thought he was insane, and the Jewish prince hardened his heart to turn aside the barbed dart of the prisoner's appeal.

For two years, Paul was a prisoner in one of the guardrooms of the old palace. But he was permitted to see and receive help from his friends. The saints in Caesarea and the surrounding area gladly ministered to him.

That period of two years was fruitful. Paul's appreciation of truth in Jesus ripened and deepened. His letters discussed less of his motives and actions and more of the believer's vital union with his Lord. They contained less doctrinal discussions of the work of Christ and more absorption in His Person, and less of the old covenant and more of the new. Those years he was restrained by the old castle walls were turned to good, because they enabled him to give the Church his priceless prison epistles.

Chapter 11

A PASSAGE TO ROME

At last Paul's term of confinement came to an end. The ecclesiastical authorities never ceased insisting that he should be handed over to their jurisdiction. But this demand, in God's good providence, was steadfastly refused by the Roman governors. They knew, and Paul knew, that such a trial could only have one end. But finally, when Festus showed signs of yielding, Paul claimed his right as a Roman citizen to have his case tried by the Emperor himself. In this way, judgment would be removed from local prejudice, and Paul would fulfill his long-cherished desire of proclaiming the gospel in Rome. As soon as possible, he was placed under the care of a centurion for transport to the imperial city.

They set sail, first in an ordinary sailing vessel, then from Myra in an Alexandrian corn ship. Contrary to Paul's advice, who even at this stage of the voyage must have been considered as a person of distinction and experience, the captain attempted to cross the open bay from the Fair Havens to

Phenice. But halfway across, the wind changed. A sudden squall struck down from the mountains and carried the big ship out to sea. Three days later, even the prisoners were called to lighten the ship by casting out cargo. After many days of the storm, in which neither sun nor moon appeared, all hope that they would be saved faded away.

Then Paul stood forth, calm and assured, with the message of God to encourage and strengthen their fainting hearts. Like Peter before his execution, the servant of God had slept quietly amid the tumult. Like Peter, too, he had been ministered to by angels. Through the thick fog, one of these ministering spirits had found his way to his side, saying, "Fear not Paul; thou must be brought before Caesar" (Acts 27:24). Evidently, the deliverance of the crew had been previously the subject of the apostle's prayer, for the angel added, "Lo, God hath given thee all they that sail with thee" (Acts 27:24). Here was an opportunity of preaching faith in God and belief in the power of prayer.

Paul detected the attempt of the sailors to get away in the lifeboat. With wisdom above common sense, he took bread, gave thanks to God in the presence of all, and began to eat. This seemed to encourage the others, and they joined him.

When they reached the shore of Malta on that dreary morning, it seemed as though nothing more could be done to further the gospel. But then a viper fell off Paul's hand without causing him harm.

The father of the chief on the island was healed of dysentery through his prayer, and diseases throughout the island were cured by his touch. The name of Jesus Christ was glorified. After some time, the travelers continued on to Rome.

Paul felt somewhat apprehensive as he at last approached the city, and the signs of her splendor and teeming life multiplied at every step. He had often thought of this moment and longed for it. Three years before, writing to the church at Rome, he said, "I long to see you, that I may impart unto you some spiritual gift" (Romans 1:11). But he had never anticipated coming like this—one of a group of prisoners led by Roman soldiers. Through his bonds, however, he was able to accomplish more than if he had been free. Had he been free, he might have gone from synagogue to synagogue, but he never would have had the opportunity of speaking to the Pretorian guard and Caesar's household.

God often answers our prayers in ways we do not expect. We may set our hearts on realizing some goal. We yearn, pray, and work for it night and day. Assurances fill our souls that one day we will rejoice in a realization of our cherished desires. But when at last we come to our Rome, we come as prisoners in chains.

God fulfilled Paul's desire to see Rome in this way probably for two reasons. First, for safety's sake, and secondly, for the wider audience that awaited him.

Do not fret at the limitations and disabilities of

your life. They constitute your opportunity. Storm and shipwreck, centurion and sea captain, soldier and chain, Caesarea and Rome—all are part of the plan and all work together for good. They will make you what you have asked to become.

Chapter 12

REDEEMED TO SERVE

Even in these days of easy and universal communication, the apostle's record as a traveler is remarkable. But how much more remarkable it appears when we recall the bandits that infested the mountain passes of Asia Minor, the rushing streams that crossed the track, the vast distances that had to be traversed on foot, the hardships of the wayside inns, and the suspicion and prejudice against the Jews.

What a record Paul has left! In his *first* missionary journey, he established churches as Christian garrisons along the central highway of Asia Minor. He preached to Jews and Gentiles, converting a proconsul and silencing a false prophet. At one time he was adored as a god, while at another time he was stoned by the same furious people. In his *second* journey, he proclaimed the gospel to Europe and established churches in some of the most famous and influential cities. Philippi, Thessalonica, Berea, Athens, and Corinth shine as beacons in the darkness.

In the *third* journey, like a Colossus, he straddled the Aegean Sea, planting one foot in Asia Minor and the other in Greece. In his *fourth* journey, after pleading his cause before at least three different tribunals, he crossed the Mediterranean, saved the crew and passengers of a storm-driven ship by his prayers and heroism, and won the respect and affection of an island of barbarians. He reached Rome in the guise of a prisoner but truly as a conqueror to unfurl the banner of his Master in the palace of the Caesars.

After his release, Paul again set forth on journeys that carried him to familiar scenes in Asia Minor and Greece. In this way he fulfilled his course until Rome and martyrdom again came in sight.

When he began his work, the world was hurrying toward its grave, in spite of what philosophy, literature, and legislation could do to arrest its moral decay. But when he was finished some thirty years later, seeds of life and salvation had been sown and nurtured into sturdy growth. These were destined, after three centuries, to displace the remnants of heathenism with the fresh undergrowth of Christian civilization.

What was Paul's secret of accomplishing this marvelous work? It was not in his intellectual talent and eloquent speech, for these were more than neutralized by his physical weaknesses—his "thorn" and his "contemptible" utterance. (See 2 Corinthians 11:6.) His source of power was the same which is within the reach of us all.

In the forefront, we must place the apostle's vivid remembrance of the mercy that had been shown him. "I obtained mercy," he wrote in 1 Timothy 1:13. He never could forget how deeply he had sinned and how strenuously he had resisted that same grace which he now proclaimed. How could he ever despair of men, since he had found mercy? How could he give up when the same grace that had saved him waited to help him?

From the beginning to the close of his career, Paul was impelled by one thought—he had been redeemed to serve. He had been saved that he might lead others to salvation. This memory was the reason for his exhausting toil. It is well for us, if we can get away for a time from the bustle and rush of life, to stand beneath the cross where Jesus died, realizing that every drop of His blood appeals to us to give our lives for the cause that cost Him His.

Paul was prepared to make any sacrifice to save men. He was equally careful to organize little Christian communities to develop the new life. But all such purposes were subordinated to his earliest epistle, "not as pleasing men, but God, which trieth our hearts" (1 Thessalonians 2:4). The outward results of his endeavors or men's opinions mattered little, as long as he knew in his heart that it pleased God. In the next epistle, he yearns "that the name of our Lord Jesus Christ may be glorified" (2 Thessalonians 1:72). We cannot forget that the passion of Christ's heart during his earthly ministry was to glorify His Father, and a similar passion burned in the heart of Paul to glorify the Son. Near the end of his ministry, that purpose grew even stronger. It was always his earnest expectation and hope that Christ should be magnified in his body, whether by life or death.

If this was our single aim, our lives would be greatly simplified. We often set out to accomplish things which, though good in themselves, fall short of God's best. When revival does not ensue and hosts of souls are not converted, we are apt to feel angry or disappointed with ourselves and God. But if we simply sought the glory of our Master, we would discover that we succeed amid apparent failure and are more than conquerors when fleeing for our lives.

Happy is the man who can face the verdict of obvious results, of his fellows, of the inner circle of dearest friends, and even of his own heart, and say, "With me it is a very small thing that I should be judged of you, or man's judgment: yea, I judge not mine own self. For I know nothing against myself; yet am I not hereby justified: but he that judgeth me is the Lord. Therefore judge nothing before the time, until the Lord come, who both will bring to light the hidden things of darkness, and will make manifest the counsels of the hearts: and then shall every man have praise from God" (1 Corinthians 4:3-5).

To each of us a stewardship is committed—of wealth, time, influence, or talent in thought and speech. Surely stewards are required, not that they would realize all their dreams but that they be found faithful to Him that appointed them. Judge your life not by results but by motives and by the smile of His good pleasure who appointed you.

Chapter 13

SECRETS OF SUCCESS

Paul's plan of living greatly contributed to his success—he had no plan at all. His way had been prepared by God before the worlds were made, and he had only to discover its track. The scheme of the temple of his life had been conceived by the divine Architect. He had only to get it by communion with God. He need do nothing but what he saw his Savior doing. His one aim was to repeat on earth what God was doing in the unseen and eternal realm.

The pattern of the Body of Christ, the position of each believer among its members, and the work which each should accomplish was fixed before the worlds were made. "Teach me to do thy will; for thou art my God: thy spirit is good, lead me into the land of uprightness" (Psalm 143:10). This should be the prayer of each Christian worker.

The secret of Paul's success lay most of all in his ability to extract power from his weaknesses. He had great gifts of character, energy, leadership, and communication. But had it not been for his infirmity, he might never have become the great apostle of the Gentiles or accomplished such splendid work. He might have yielded to self-confidence and relied on these extraordinary endowments, instead of casting himself absolutely, as he was compelled to do, on the power of God. His life work was accomplished not by himself but by God operating through his frail, mortal body. As a vessel prepared for the Master's use, he became utterly dependent on the Master's hand to direct and empower him.

In early life, he was one of Gamaliel's most promising pupils—strong, self-reliant, clear in thought, incisive in speech, and swift in action. Among the men of his age, few could match Saul of Tarsus who became a member of the Jewish Sanhedrin early in his career. Would anyone recognize him in the weakness, fear, and trembling of this broken man? Because he was weak, he was strong. Because he wore chains, he was the great emancipator from chains. Because he was poor, he succeeded in making many rich.

The only thing we need to know is whether we have been called by God to accomplish certain work for Him. Then, if limitations and hindrances suggest the impossibility of ever accomplishing it, let us dare to glory in them. Let us do by faith the work which others do by human might.

Another element in the success of the apostle's work must be found in his self-denial. He had liberal views of truth and life and could probably have done many things which he carefully shunned, lest his influence for Christ be impaired. In 1 Corinthians 8:13 he tells us that if meat offended his brother, he would never eat it. As far as his own conscience was concerned, he could eat in an idol's temple without condemnation; yet he dare not do it, lest he should cast a stumbling block before a weak disciple.

He carefully kept his body under subjection so that he would do the utmost possible for the souls of men and keep the Lord from choosing another instrument more suited for His purpose. "Giving no offence in any thing, that the ministry be not blamed" (2 Corinthians 6:3).

This, too, is a path in which we may follow the steps of this great servant of Jesus. All Christian workers, zealous for the coming of God's Kingdom, must give up indulgences and practices that are not in themselves unlawful but may hinder souls. In determining our actions regarding to the effect upon others, some matters lie in the grey areas between what is clearly defined as right and wrong. The more widespread our influence over souls, the more we must consider the effect our actions will have on others.

Let us not forget the eloquence of Paul's tears. "Remember," he said to the elders of the Ephesian church, "that by the space of three years I ceased not to warn every one night and day with tears" (Acts 20:31). Not content with appealing to them by day, he preached at night also. He did not cease this ministry for three long years but pursued it without relaxation, interruption, or pause. This work was not done with the persistence of a zealot or the eagerness of a partisan but with the tears of a soul-lover.

Why is it that this fountain of tears seems to be denied us? We have tears for all things other than the infinite loss of those who have rejected the gospel. In losing the power of tears, we have lost one great power of causing them. It is by broken hearts that hearts are broken, and by wet eyes that eyes are made to brim over with the waters of repentant sorrow.

Lastly, let us not forget the apostle's individual interest in his converts. He warned every one of them night and day with tears. "Whom we preach, warning *every man,* and teaching *every man* in all wisdom; that we may present *every man* perfect in Christ Jesus" (Colossians 1:28). How he dwells on that phrase, "every man"! He had no use for the reckless haste that shakes the boughs of the fruit trees to obtain their precious harvest. He knew too well the peril of injuring the delicate bloom. All the fruit he gathered for God was hand-picked. One soul for whom Christ died was, in his sight, of unspeakable worth.

Underlying all these was the fundamental concept that it was not he, but the grace and power of God that worked in and through him. He did not work for Christ but offered himself to Him without reserve. Christ shone in the inmost recesses of Paul's being. Then he could go forth to illuminate the hearts of men. His one desire was to yield himself

267

to God and that his members might be used as weapons in the great conflict against the powers of hell.

This is, after all, the first and last lesson for the Christian worker. Be clean, pure of heart, and simple in motive. See to it that no friction stands between your will and Christ's. Subdue your own activities as much as your own natural laziness. Believe that God will accomplish in you the greatest results possible to the capacity of your nature. Let there be no thought of what you can do for God but only of what God can do through you. Nothing will make you as intense and ceaseless in your activity as this.

This brings an end to cowardice because you will find yourself carried along by an irresistible impulse. It also brings an end to pride because you will have no occasion to boast. "Shall the axe boast itself against him that heweth therewith? or shall the saw magnify itself against him that shaketh it?" (Isaiah 10:15).

These words apply to us all. God judges, not by the character but by the spirit of our work; not by its extent but by its depth; not by results but by the spirit that animates and inspires.

We may be certain of the gracious cooperation of the Holy Spirit. Whenever His servants stand up to speak, the Spirit of God bears witness to their words. Wherever they bear witness, whether by words or actions, the results testify to His mighty presence and power. And whenever they cross the threshold of some new soul, home, or land, men become aware that the gospel has come to them—not in word only but also in power, in the Holy Spirit, and in much assurance. May we also live, testify, and minister, that we may be good stewards of God's grace, co-workers with God, and ambassadors through whom God may call men to be reconciled to Himself.

Chapter 14

ENTRANCE INTO GLORY

Paul was treated with great leniency when he arrived in Rome. This was due to the providence of God and the kind intervention of the centurion who had developed a sincere admiration for him during these months of travel together. He was permitted to rent a house near the great Pretorian barracks and live under house arrest. The only sign of his captivity was the chain that fastened his wrist to a Roman soldier.

There were many advantages in this arrangement. It protected him from the hatred of his people. It also gave him a marvelous opportunity of casting the seeds of the gospel into the rivers of a population that poured from the metropolis throughout the known world.

At the same time, it must have been very frustrating. He always had to be in the presence of one who was filled with Gentile aversion to Jewish habits and pagan irresponsiveness to Christian fervor. He could make no movement without the clanking of his chain and the consent of his custodian. His conferences, his prayers, and the writing of his epistles had to be done beneath emotionless eyes or amid brutal and blasphemous interruptions. All this must have been excessively trying to a sensitive temperament like Paul's.

This difficult lesson taught him to be content even with this for the sake of the gospel. But this, too, he could do through Christ that strengthened him. Many of those brawny soldiers became humble, earnest disciples. With a glow of holy joy, he informed the Philippians that his bonds in Christ had become manifest throughout the whole Pretorian guard.

Three days after his arrival in Rome, Paul summoned the leaders of the synagogues. (See Acts 28:17.) The Jews were the objects of the dislike and ridicule of the imperial city. At the first interview, they cautiously expressed the wish to hear and judge for themselves concerning the sect which had been denounced by all other Jews.

At the second meeting, after listening to Paul's explanations and appeals for an entire day, there was the usual division of opinion. "Some believed the things which were spoken, and some believed not" (Acts 28:24). According to his usual practice, his testimony was first offered to his own people. Now no further obstacle remained to his addressing a wider audience. The message of salvation was sent to the Gentiles. For the next two years, his accusers prepared their case against him. Meanwhile Paul "received all that came in unto him, Preaching the kingdom of God, and teaching those things which concern the Lord Jesus Christ, with all confidence, no man forbidding him'' (Acts 28:28).

It is almost certain that Paul was acquitted at his first trial and permitted for at least two or three years to engage again in his beloved work. He was evidently expecting to be released when he wrote to the Philippians: "I trust in the Lord that I also myself shall come shortly" (Philippians 2:24). In his letter to Philemon also, he asked that a lodging be prepared for him because he hoped that their prayer for his return would soon be granted. (See Philemon 22.)

Whether his liberation was due to the help of the centurion or to more explicit reports received from Caesarea, history does not record; but it was by the decree of Someone greater than Nero that the chain was removed from the apostle's wrist, and he was free to go.

Once more a free man, Paul visited Philemon and the church of Colossae. Then he made his way to the church at Ephesus to converse further with them on the sacred mysteries which he had begun to unfold in his epistle. Leaving Timothy behind with the injunction to command some that they should preach no other gospel than they had heard from his lips, he traveled onward to Macedonia and Philippi.

What a greeting must have been given to him there! They were his beloved brethren, his joy and crown. Lydia and Clement, Euodia and Syntyche,

Epaphroditus and the jailer, together with many other fellow-workers whose names are in the Book of Life, must have gathered around to minister to his frail, worn body and be inspired by his heroic soul.

From Philippi he passed to other churches in Greece, including Corinth. Finally he set sail with Titus for Crete where he left him to set things in order and appoint elders in every city. (See Titus 1:5.) On his return to the mainland, he wrote a letter to Titus in which he implied that he was about to spend the winter at Nicopolis, surrounded by several friends. They gladly helped him strengthen and purify the teaching in these young churches. Each of the churches probably had to pass through the phases of doctrinal and practical difficulty reflected in Paul's letters to Corinth. (See 1 Corinthians 3:12-13.)

This blessed liberty, however, was soon cut short. One of the most terrible events in the history of the ancient world—the burning of Rome—took place in the year A.D. 64. To divert the suspicion from himself, Nero accused the Christians of causing the blaze. Immediately the fierce flames of the first general persecution broke out. Those who lived in the metropolis, and who must have been well known and dear to Paul, were seized and subjected to horrible torture. Meanwhile a strict search was made throughout the empire for their leaders. It was not likely that an eminent a Christian as Paul would escape.

He was staying for a time at Troas. His arrest was sudden, giving him no time to gather up his precious books and parchments. He was forced to leave behind the copies of his epistles, a Hebrew Bible, and some early copies of the sayings of our Lord. A little group of faithful friends accompanied him in this last sad journey. For the second time, Paul reached Rome.

The circumstances of his second imprisonment differed greatly from those of the first. Then he had his own house; now he was left in close confinement. Then he was easily accessible; now his friends had to seek him out diligently, and it took some courage to visit him in the prison. Then he was the center of a large circle of friends and sympathizers; now adversity had greatly thinned their ranks, while others had been dispatched on distant missions. "Only Luke is with me" (2 Timothy 4:11) is the rather sad expression of the old man's loneliness. Then he cherished a bright hope of speedy liberation; now accusations against him included the charge of introducing new customs hostile to the stability of the imperial government. The vagueness made it impossible to combat, and it was inevitable that he would be caught within its meshes.

The time had come for him to release the anchor and set sail. But it caused him no sorrow. He had set his heart on being clothed with the body that was from heaven and on being suddenly caught up to be forever with the Lord. Not by the triumphant path of the air but by the dark path of a martyr's death would he pass into the presence of the Lord. The avenue of his home-going was, however, of small importance. He was only too thankful, on his review of his career, to say humbly and truthfully, "I have fought a good fight, I have finished my course, I have kept the faith: Henceforth there is laid up for me a crown of righteousness" (2 Timothy 4:7-8).

What happened during Paul's trial? How long was he kept in suspense? Did Timothy arrive in time to see him and to be with him at the last moment? What was the exact method of his martyrdom? To these questions, there is no certain reply. Tradition points to a spot about three miles from Rome, on the Ostian road, where he was beheaded. As his spirit left its frail tenement, he entered the house not made with hands, eternal in the heavens.

His was now the inheritance of the saints in light, of which the Holy Spirit had been the promise and first-fruit. He had passed the goal and had attained to the prize of his high calling in Christ. He had been found in Christ, not having his own righteousness but the righteousness which is of God by faith. As he gave the account of his stewardship, who can doubt that the Lord greeted him with, "Well done, good and faithful servant; enter into the joy of the Lord."

Among those who eagerly anticipate that hour when the Bridegroom will present the Church to Himself without spot or wrinkle, there is none more eager than Paul! He looked constantly for the appearance of the glorious Savior and did much to prepare the Church for her Lord! Among the stones of the foundations of the New Jerusalem, on which are written the names of the twelve apostles of the Lamb, will surely be found that of Saul, also called Paul. He was formerly a blasphemer and a persecutor, but he obtained mercy and remained faithful to the end.

ABOUT THE AUTHOR

F.B. Meyer was one of the most knowledgeable and influential scholars of the late nineteenth and early twentieth centuries.

Born in England in 1847, Dr. Meyer accepted the Lord as a child. "Put Thy Holy Spirit in me to make my heart good, like Jesus Christ was," the five-year-old prayed. The Lord honored this youthful zeal, and F.B. Meyer's life became a constant interchange between Master and servant, Father and son.

Dr. Meyer authored over seventy books and thirty-five booklets. In addition, he edited several magazines *(Worship and Work, Christian Treasure, etc.)* and wrote prefaces for over twenty literary works. He is chiefly remembered for his Bible biographies, three of which are contained in this volume.

Besides these extensive literary endeavors, Dr. Meyer held pastorates in Leicester, York, and London. His ministry also included traveling worldwide, preaching and teaching from his extensive knowledge of the Scriptures.

Meyer's friendship with the famous soul-winner, D.L. Moody, sparked a new phase of evangelism in the author's life. As a result, the Lord used him to bring many people to Christ.

Dr. F.B. Meyer went to be with the Lord in 1929 at the age of eighty-two. His saintly life is an inspiration to us, and his books should be treasured not only as a testimony of a godly man but as a guide to a godly life.